WONDERFULLY COMPOSED

WONDERFULLY COMPOSED

A Musical Guide to Emotional Expression

Tom Pierce

Illustrated by
Ray Heilman

Wonderfully Composed
by Tom Pierce
Copyright ©2019 Wonderfully Composed LLC

All rights reserved. This book is protected under the copyright laws of the United States of America. This book may not be copied or reprinted for commercial gain or profit.

ISBN 978-1-7341740-0-7

*This book is dedicated to my wife,
without whom I would not have had the courage
to express my deepest thoughts.*

*I will give thanks to you,
For I am fearfully and wonderfully made;
Wonderful are Your works,
And my soul knows it very well.
(Psalm 139:14, New American Standard Bible)*

Contents

Preface iii
Acknowledgements v
Introduction: The Way of Music ix

Section I: Your Instrument 1
Find Your Voice 4
Set Your Pace 10
Free Your Spirit 17
Learn Your Limits 28

Section II: Your Notes 37
C - Confessing Love 41
C# - The Point of Fear 47
D - Daring to Desire 53
D# - The Shadow of Sorrow 59
E - Entering into Joy 69
F - Finding Courage 79
F# - The Speed of Anger 85
G - Grasping Peace 93
G# - The Cup of Loneliness 101
A - Approaching Intimacy 109
A# - The Knots Of Anxiety 119
B – Building Upon Gratitude 129
C – Composing Love 139

Section III: Your Part 147
Harmony: The Art of Blending 152
Symphony: The Need for Belonging 159
Community: The Power of Binding......................165

PREFACE

"Don't let anyone tell you how to grieve."

I heard my wife offer this simple, timeless admonition to a friend who had suffered a recent loss, and my heart was strengthened. She has a way of expressing, in very few words, deep and powerful truths that would take me volumes to unearth. Brevity indeed inhabits the soul of her wit, and it is exactly that gift which inspires me most — that capacity to express clearly what matters most, while simultaneously liberating and enabling others to express themselves freely as well, without fear of judgment or threat of critique, full of confidence that their unrefined offerings will be received as valid, valuable, and vibrantly significant.

In writing this book, I aspire to do what she does (albeit with significantly more words): to encourage you to give authentic voice to the full spectrum of all you know and feel, to practice the art of creative revelation, and to enrich the world around you with the unparalleled beauty of your unique experience.

Tom

ACKNOWLEDGEMENTS

Each of us has been influenced by a great many mentors, teachers, writers, and friends. After a number of years of processing and integrating their inspiration, it is often difficult to remember exactly where a certain thought was first learned, or a given phrase first heard. The very process of putting this book together has led me back nostalgic roads to many of the people whose legacies I hope to honor. Here I wish to join you in expressing enduring gratitude to all those who have guided our learning, taught us their ways, and shown us pathways of wisdom, that we might walk in them.

Mrs. Ruth Peal Graf, my eleventh grade English teacher, was hands down the most demanding teacher I had yet encountered. Her exacting standards were intimidating, yet she had a remarkably pleasant way of holding both herself and her students to those standards, and took quite seriously her mission to teach and guide us every step of the way up that steep ascent. The research paper she demanded of all her juniors was a rite of passage; the level of expectation for research and attribution — not to mention grammar, spelling, and artfulness of expression (or diction) — was as rigorous as any I encountered later in college or even in graduate school. I did my paper on Dr. Norman Vincent Peale, whom I admired deeply.

Mrs. Graf took joy in telling me that Dr. Peale's wife was also named Ruth, and thus shared her maiden name. She did not take joy in telling me that my writing was too dry, too technical, and lacked creative or artistic character. It hurt when she said, quite transparently and bluntly, that she did not believe I would ever be a good writer, although I might be quite good at other things. She may have said that in part because she knew it would motivate and challenge me, which it certainly has. She may have been simply honest, wishing only to give me the kind of feedback that might provide the truest form of guidance. It did that as well; I later chose mathematics as my major, and have worked as a systems analyst for most of my career. In that field, my precise technical writing has proven to be a strength, yet I have always nurtured a deep desire to someday develop a more creative style.

Mrs. Sue Neuen was the music teacher, boldly and energetically establishing a new music and choral program at the school. She heard me speak at assembly one morning, and approached me afterwards with words I would not forget. She assured me that if I could speak that clearly in a public setting, that she could teach me to sing clearly as well. I doubted that sincerely, for all my prior efforts to sing – in church choirs, with friends, or with the bluegrass band in which I played banjo – produced only a painfully strained, unpleasant whisper, with an occasional burst of what could best be described as a muffled off-key shout. I can't explain why I trusted her, but I did. I signed up for her chorus, and made some good friends among that group. I also signed up for her Music Theory class, on the faint hope that my background with ukulele, banjo, and guitar might somehow translate into a better understanding of music in a broader sense. She was an amazing teacher and leader, and I completely thrived in her class. The mathematics behind music theory amazed me, as did her astounding insight that the "rules" of music were made to be broken. She saw the rules and traditions of music theory and musical expression as dotted-line guides, intended only to provide general bearings, particularly to those who most creatively enjoyed transcending them. She was such a person. She pushed boundaries, explored uncharted pathways, tried things that might not work, and led her students on unforgettable journeys.

I needed both of them, really, Mrs. Graf and Mrs. Neuen. I needed both the exacting standards and the unorthodox drive. I needed both the challenge and the inspiration. I needed to learn both my limitations and my possibilities. I still need both of those things, perhaps now more than ever before. It is my hope that by sharing a dozen or so stories from my own adventure, I might offer you an opportunity to glimpse some of your own potential. The jury is out on whether I might ever become a good writer, but thanks to the encouragement of good people, I'm going to give it a try.

A special word of gratitude is owed to my dear friend and gifted illustrator, Ray Heilman. Ray's talents are remarkably diverse, from computer software to music and art and many realms beyond. In each facet, Ray exhibits an extraordinary authenticity and guileless purity of soul, which makes him not only easy to trust but also a seemingly inexhaustible source of support, guidance, and humble inspiration. I trust that you are able to see in the creativity of his illustrations something of the depth of understanding and spiritual perception that makes him extraordinary.

I would also like to thank my trusted advisor, Scott Couchenour. My conversations with Scott have long been a vehicle for clarity and inspiration when I have needed it most. Many of the best thoughts and ideas articulated in this book were cultivated and brought into focus through interaction with his fertile mind, and encouraged by his steadfast heart. He is my coach, my partner, and my friend.

INTRODUCTION: THE WAY OF MUSIC

Music is a gift, both to performer and to audience. It provides ways to say things without words, to share passions without censors, to seek depths without danger, to reveal character without explanation. It also provides abundant wisdom about the nature of our mysterious connection to each other, and about our capacity to live our lives intertwined with the melodies and harmonies that surround and transcend us. I have known many musicians who shared more deeply of themselves through their hands and fingers than they ever did with mouth and tongue. I have been inspired more richly by soaring orchestrations than ever by argument or philosophy. I have been brought to tears by simple, pristine melody in ways unmatched by poem or prose. Yet here am I, attempting to use words and phrases to express what I hear most clearly in my heart. The effort will undoubtedly be incomplete, and at best a hint or nudge in the direction of true beauty. Nevertheless, I write.

A wise choral conductor once taught me that there is no such thing as written music. Anything made of paper that claims to be music is simply a suggestion — a series of annotations intended to guide musicians in the manifestations of their own unique gifts. In order to become music, a song simply must be sung or played, transformed into audible expression – whether for the ears of a vast and appreciative audience, for the private satisfaction of only the musician, or for the one singular audience deemed most worthy of such a worshipful offering. The expression and experience of music are thus inextricably intertwined, and symbiotically composed. As such, I believe that music is quite an apt reflection of the emotional composition of our souls. Any separation between our experience and our expression is a distortion of our authentic selves, and a form of deception to the world around us. Any disregard for the experience of the people around us is callous and destructive, and an abusive waste of our most precious gifts. We learn authentic, sensitive self-expression in much the same way that musicians learn music: haltingly and timidly at first, fluidly and openly with practice, masterfully and beautifully in time.

SECTION I: YOUR INSTRUMENT

The first instrument I learned to play was a ukulele. My Dad travelled quite a bit with the Tennessee Air National Guard, and on a trip to Hawaii when I was about eight, he brought back the Kamaka ukulele that hangs on my office wall today, over fifty years later. The neck came loose from the body many years ago, but after a few failed attempts at repair, the glue seems to be holding now. My teacher was a gentle-spirited man named Tommy Covington, and I remember his kindness and patience. He not only gave me a wonderful introduction to the ukulele, and through it the wonderful world of musical practice, but also provided me my first exposure to musical performance. In the fairly early days of television, he had his own live show on a local station. After clearing it with my mother, he invited me to come to the studio one Saturday, and had me play one song "on the air". I vaguely remember him asking me a few questions on camera after I played, but I felt so painfully shy that I think my answers hardly surpassed a few soft syllables. (I have recently read that his studio was also the site, not many years earlier, of one of the first broadcasts of a talented local singer by the name of Dolly Parton. It is indeed a small world.)

About two years later, I was ready to tackle another string. I told my dad I would like to learn to play the five-string banjo. He picked up what we jokingly referred to as a "cardboard throwaway model", just to see if I was serious. He also found me a teacher, Wayne

Goforth, a classical guitarist who had never played banjo before, but who was willing to learn in order to teach me. And yes, he taught me classical arrangements for the five-string banjo as a foundation, before moving on to Scruggs-style bluegrass ballads, rags, and folk songs. After five years of enthusiastic practice (and occasional performances at school talent shows), I was deemed ready for a better banjo: a Baldwin Ode Model C that I treasured for many years. (It has since been replaced with a very fine Gibson Mastertone.)

I joined a small bluegrass band in high school, and began to learn the art of playing well with others, in the musical sense. I soon discovered that I needed to learn how to play guitar as well, if for no other reason than to communicate with guitarists (who often struggled to communicate with banjo pickers). Wayne was kind enough to teach me both classical and bluegrass guitar, and my generous father furnished an absolutely beautiful 1968 Conde Hermanos Flamenco guitar that he bought on a trip to Madrid. A confession is in order here: while I have known all along that it was a fabulous instrument, I had not until this writing truly examined the label inside the body, or learned anything about its maker. Now I am stunned, realizing for the first time what an incredibly valuable instrument I have been given, and what a tremendous honor it has been to carry it with me, and share its music, through all these years.

FIND YOUR VOICE

You have been given an incredibly valuable instrument. There never has been, there never will be, another like you on the face of this earth. As is true of each snowflake, you are utterly unique. Your experience, the sum total of all that you have seen and heard, is unlike the accumulated experience of any other. The emotional character and complexity of your soul is unequalled and unparalleled. The way you express your emotions is unique as well. Whether you find your authentic style though a stringed instrument, a drum set, a sketch pad, a keyboard, or your own vocal cords, no one will ever share their thoughts and feelings quite the way you do. Far too many people try to be or imitate someone else, to the neglect of their own distinctive design and abilities.

To express yourself well, it may seem obvious that you must first know yourself well. And yet something rather counter-intuitive is at work here. Much (perhaps most) of what we come to know about ourselves is learned in large part through our trial-and-error adventures in communicating with others, in various awkward efforts to make ourselves heard and understood, and in a perpetual quest to connect with people who seem to see what we see, hear what we hear, and feel what we feel. We learn from the way people respond to us, as much as we learn from our own reactions to other people. We imitate as much as we differentiate; our desire to know our own uniqueness is just as strong as our desire to be included, both among those who are much like us and among those who are not. Our journeys in self-expression and self-understanding are thus inevitably connected, and inseparably linked.

But what forms the substance of this bridge between knowing yourself and expressing yourself? It seems like it should be obvious, doesn't it? Is it made up simply of authenticity, granting yourself full permission to be who you are, to acknowledge your own experience, and allow your expression to flow freely from genuine emotion? Surely that is the foundation of the bridge, but there seems to be something more. Is there not also a need to consider thoughtfully how we will impact others, a legitimate desire not to harm or offend, and a social duty of sorts to bring light and inspiration – rather than unfiltered noise – to the table of shared experience? Do the distinctions in how we share our thoughts derive directly from our decisions about self-disclosure, from the willful revealing and concealing of various parts of what we know and feel? I believe that there is something inherently unique in what happens within us — in the internal processing and integration of our experiences and emotions — that gives us each our distinctive tone. We become readily recognizable to others not only by how we look or what we say, but by how we sound, and how we come across. As surely as an infant recognizes its mother's voice, or as sheep recognize the voice of their shepherd, we learn the voice and tone of the people we know well, and we become known by ours.

Your particular blend of personality traits is a part of your dynamic design, the way that you have been shaped and formed throughout your own history, from cellular differentiation to social interaction, as well as the way you continue to shape and mold yourself, and select the pathways of your own growth. Your personality will not dictate which emotions you experience, or how deeply. A vast range of emotional events are for the most part inevitable, and largely unforeseeable. Seeking immunity from their impact is simply futile. However, your unique disposition will govern how, when, and to whom you express your emotions, and how those expressions will be perceived by others.

There is something that happens in between the experience and the expression of emotion, something that affects how it sounds, if and when it comes out. When you strike the strings of a ukulele, a banjo, or a guitar, similar soundwaves are formed at first, but something different happens within the body of each instrument, something that transforms those waves into distinctive tones. Their resonators are different – in substance, form, and depth. So it is with flutes and bagpipes: the same breath may enter in, but that wind is transformed before it moves to the listener's ear. Our temperaments are the resonators of emotional transformation, the hidden internal processes by which the raw materials of common experience are molded into our own unique expression.

Authenticity always needs to be balanced with sensitivity. When our expression is merely a presentation of how we think we are supposed to feel, or of how we wish to be perceived, then it is phony. It does not ring true in the ears of our listeners, and fails to either enlighten or inspire. But when it is authentic— transparently revealing not only our experience but also the distinctive ways in which those experiences take shape within us — then what comes out is creative in the truest sense, and most richly valuable to those who hear and understand. By the same token, when our internal processing is focused only inward, without respect or regard for others, then it becomes insensitive, stale, and toxic to those around us. But when our inner interpretations are attentive to our full context — the impact of our experience on the lives of other people involved, as well as ourselves — then the output is not only distinctively ours but also lovingly shared. When both transparency and compassion are clearly conveyed, the integrity of the creative event is robust, enduring, and sound.

This is what I think is meant by finding your voice: knowing the sound — and the soundness — of your own self-expression. This is how we go about revealing our character, to those who have ears to hear, and a genuine desire to listen.

SET YOUR PACE

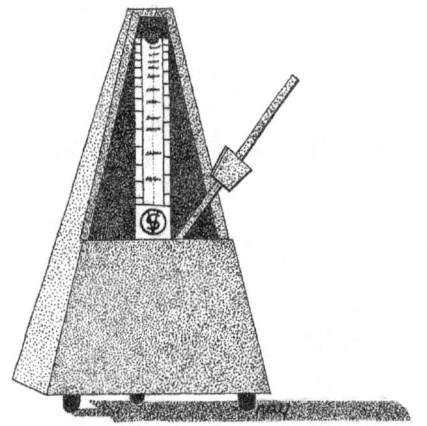

I'm not going to tell you to slow down, and I'm not going to tell you to speed up. The main reason for that is that I don't have a clue how fast you are going now... and even if I did, I wouldn't know how fast you want or need to be going. What I do know is that all of us struggle from time to time on how best to manage our time.

It seems to work best when our pace blends well with the pace of the people around us. My work is about an hour away from home, and I spend about two hours a day driving. Honestly, I can't tell which annoys me more: people who drive too fast, or people who drive too slowly. The speed demons ride my bumper, dart in and out of tight spaces, and make me nervous whenever they're around me. The slow pokes get in everybody's way, cause bottlenecks in otherwise clear traffic, test my patience, and raise anxiety of a completely different kind. If we could all just agree on a common speed — generally somewhere between the speed limit posted and the one enforced — travel would be much more pleasant.

When I directed the community choir, it was my job (some would say my only job) to set the tempo for each song. But there is a lot more to setting a good tempo than picking a speed and waving your arms. The choir always sang with more energy and enthusiasm when the pace was fast, but the harmonies were more beautiful and lyrical when we slowed it down a bit. On complex pieces, the instrumentalists would make more mistakes at higher speeds, but the drummer would get bored if the tempo dragged. (Trust me — nobody wants a bored drummer in the house.) Truth be told, the drummer was pretty sure it was his job to set the pace, and the choir tended to follow his lead more than mine. (Side note: if you think you're leading but nobody's following, you're just taking a lonely walk.) I found it wise to collaborate with the drummer ahead of time.

It is in fact all about time. And to answer the ageless musical question: no, I don't think anybody truly knows what time it is, and not too many people really even care. The Smithsonian has a very impressive exhibit on the history of timekeeping devices, yet not a one of them can actually keep any time; time keeps on slipping away, despite their best efforts. And all of the advanced time-saving technology fails to help us save any time at all; at the end of the day, there still isn't any left. All we can do with time is spend it, and we all spend it at the same rate, no matter what technique we employ. Many a hurried coworker has pleaded, "Give me a minute"; but every minute I have ever had was gone before I could figure out how to give it to anybody.

YOUR TIME

But there was this one time... after driving about nine hours in traffic moving both too fast and too slow, when all I wanted to do was buy a few hours of sleep at a peaceful hotel, but only after finding a spot to get a quick, long-overdue bite to eat. It was far past dinner time, and past closing time for most of the restaurants I passed. At last I found a place still open, with a few minutes to spare before they locked the doors. The hostess seated me immediately, and the waitress arrived too promptly, for I had not yet had time to process either the menu or my appetite, much less the intersection where the two might meet. Seemingly sensing my rushed frustration, my waitress gave me a surprisingly timely and welcome piece of advice. "Take your time", she said, and her gentle words penetrated deeply into my otherwise frantic soul. I took her advice; I took my time. It was indeed a gift, and in that moment I was able to receive it with gratitude. I found something on the menu that sounded good, and I took my time enjoying every bite. I even took the time to indulge in dessert, and enjoyed sharing a generous tip with my wise waitress and advisor.

As the preacher said, there is a time for everything, a time for every activity under the sun. The only thing required of us is to recognize the right time, and to take it. Take your time. Take the time that has been given to you, the time that fits the things you want or need to do, the time that is right where it needs to be, right when it needs to be there.

Sometimes you'll choose to walk, other times to run, and still other times to stand quietly still, perhaps in awe and wonder at the wonderful time you are having. Choose the pace that fits your moment, grab hold of your elusive present, and take it. Claim it as your very own, for that is exactly what it is: your time.

YOUR SPACE

You do not need to understand Einstein's Theory of Relativity to know that there is a remarkable relationship between time and space. Your selection of pace is completely intertwined with your recognition of place. My mother taught me not to run in church, and although I had little comprehension of that restriction in my childhood, it now seems instinctive not to rush through holy places. In drivers' education I learned to slow down in the presence of a funeral procession, out of basic respect for the grieving. In the mountains of east Tennessee I learned to slow down on tight curves, whether or not road signs so ordered, simply as a matter of safety and self-preservation. In

Army training I was taught to move with a purpose, to march to a cadence, and to run with endurance. In tennis I can chase the ball with reckless abandon, but I have learned that it is wise to slow down before meeting the fence. It is always good to match speed with purpose, to move quickly when destination matters more than travel, but slowly when the journey itself is the object of desire. Let the place that you are in guide the pace of your movement.

Margins matter. Reserve for yourself the space and the time to move freely and breathe. Maintain the personal distance you need, and do not hesitate to withdraw from crowds when your soul requires solitude. Push back against unwelcome intrusions; defend your boundaries with diligence; give honor and homage due to sacred paths in which you walk. Many have walked this way before you came, and many will follow after you leave. Leave for them a trail and a space in which they can walk freely and live abundantly. Brush away the barriers, smooth out the rough patches, and always leave a place better than you found it.

My wife and I both find deep replenishment in watching water move. Whether it be the rhythmic tides of the Atlantic sweeping a sandy beach, the mighty roar of Kentucky's Cumberland Falls (the Niagara of the South), or the mesmerizing tranquility of a mountain stream meandering through the Great Smoky Mountains, we cannot help but be captivated by their relentless power and majestic grace. They move at their own paces and claim their own spaces in ways that transform our understanding of life itself. In doing so, they bring life with them, wherever they go.

Move through time and space at your own pace, on a path of your own choosing. Be relentless in your journey, and gracious at every step.

FREE YOUR SPIRIT

There is a flow to life that extends beyond speed, beyond time and distance, into a realm that is more easily sensed than measured. The flow of energy throughout your body, the flow of interaction in your relationships, even the flow of your presence within the spaces you inhabit constitute a complexity of forces that none of us completely understands, yet all of us seem to experience, sometimes very deeply. You know when you are "in sync" with the world around you, and when you are not. You can tell when your mind, body, and spirit are "on the same page", and when they are "out of whack". Being "out of sorts" appears to be a universal phenomenon, a recognizable disorder, a describable dysfunction, and an incredibly common "dis-ease": the state of being not "at ease", not at peace, not well, not good.

What does "good" feel like? What does it feel like when you are firing on all cylinders, when all the gears are meshing, all the joints are lubricated, all the engines are fueled up and the tires are hugging the road? It feels vibrant. It feels alive. It feels free. In the most universal and broadly understood sense of the word, it feels like love. Love, as the relational energy that binds us to each other – and even to those before and beyond our time – invigorates our being and energizes our hopes and dreams. When love gets stuck, everything in our complex internal and external systems feels the impact, and suffers the constraint. When love flows freely, life is good and abundant, and the world around us is both blessing and blessed, for we see and hear that we are part of a vast and eternal flow of light, of life, and of love.

YOUR TIMING

If you are alive, you have a pulse. If you are living, you have rhythm. I know, there are many who seem to have no natural sense of rhythm or timing whatsoever. (The other banjo player in my high school bluegrass band sometimes suspected that I was among them.) To some of us, dancing is by definition awkward, devoid of any intuitive notion that might synchronize our movements with any music, or our footsteps with those of any partner. To some of us, the simple act of repeating a joke seems pointless, for the punchline seems always to arrive too early or too late, with too little energy applied in the setup and too much wasted in tardy explanation. To some of us, every swing of the bat misses the ball not only in space, but even more in time. Our timing is just off. Our curiosity drives questions at times deemed inappropriate, our shared thoughts catch people off guard, our contributions come across as interruptions. Even our thoughtful silence is often mistimed, and misconstrued as distance or disinterest.

Nevertheless, there is a rhythm to everything that we do. Inhaling and exhaling occur at intervals that form a discernible pattern. Sleeping and waking fall within some limited range of possibilities. Eating and drinking occur at some sustainable frequency. If you are living, these patterns repeat and recur, and are typically more noticed when a pattern is disturbed than when it is followed. You have routines and ruts, and the distinction between the two is determined largely by how happy you are to be in them.

There are also larger patterns, common in their presence, yet individual in their experience. Weekdays and weekends offer contrasting challenges. Paydays and payment due dates dictate financial flows, as other monthly cycles regulate energy and strength, pain and renewal. Seasons strike differently in the hemispheres and temperate zones, yet mark the planetary fluctuations with remarkable predictability. Annual expectations blend into generational traditions, and before long we find ourselves contemplating rhythms whose lengths far exceed our lifespans. Astronomers estimate that a single repeating rotation of our Milky Way galaxy — one galactic year — takes 250 million terrestrial years. That's far more than I know how to imagine.

Living — being alive, sustaining life, reproducing life — is itself a rhythmic pattern, made up of an infinite number of smaller rhythmic patterns, contained within an infinite number of larger rhythmic patterns. Every heartbeat extends the pattern, reinforces the rhythm, and grants us one more instant of time in which to work on our timing. And all of us need to work on our timing.

My father had a Swiss watch embedded in his soul, or something like it. He was a pilot, and a trainer of pilots. Every flight had a flight plan, and every step of that plan was timed with precision. Dad never needed an alarm clock. If he needed to wake up earlier than usual, he would simply decide the night before what time he needed to wake up, and would somehow always wake up at that time. As best I can recall, for most of my childhood breakfast was served promptly at 6am and dinner promptly at 6pm. Lateness was not treated lightly, and earliness was entirely unnecessary. Everything seemed to have its own proper schedule, and everything seemed typically to happen on time.

I did not inherit my father's watch. Once I was on my own in college, my schedule became erratic. Morning classes were mostly avoided and frequently slept through. Assignments were often started after midnight, and sleep was regularly deferred. The "all-nighter" was my trademark, with 13 occurrences counted in my freshman year alone. I despised timed tests and sought the untimed "take home" variety whenever offered. My papers were routinely late, with points subtracted accordingly. In one philosophy class, I turned in a term paper several days after the semester was over, travelling with trepidation to the home of my esteemed professor to beg his acceptance, with whatever penalties applied. I was greeted at the door by his 90-year old mother, who graciously interceded on my behalf. With compassionate humor she shared that "Bobby" — my esteemed professor, Dr. Robert Helm — was always late turning in his papers to his publishers. I was greatly relieved, and silently entertained, by her grace.

My pattern continued, forming a rhythm of its own, even through four years of service in the US Army. I know, it isn't supposed to work like that. I received my share of well-deserved reprimands, but also had the great fortune to be assigned to a position under a commanding officer whose clock worked much like mine. We both worked quite a lot — sixty to eighty hours per week was not uncommon — but we worked when we were alert, slept when we were tired, ate when we were hungry, and went home when the day's work was done. Not exactly a Swiss watch, but a rhythm that worked nonetheless.

Whatever rhythms and patterns fit your soul, don't let them become overly rigid, or recklessly chaotic. Like a skyscraper designed to sway a few inches in the wind to avoid collapse, our lives need to be designed with sway, with margin to adjust to the unpredictable. We need the flexibility to improvise, to change direction a bit when the winds and waves shift around us, but also the discipline to stay anchored in a storm. Avoid the common pretense of time management. Time itself cannot be managed; the spin and orbit of the earth are beyond our influence or control. But just as we manage the effect of the sun with sunscreen, we manage the effect of time by leveraging our energy. How we spend the energy we have is a perpetual series of conscious choices. Learn the sources and sinks of your energy supply; get to know what fuels your soul and what saps your strength. Let the music within you guide your steps, with light feet and gracious humor. Bounce the eraser on your desk; tap your fingers on the steering wheel and your toes on the office floor. Feel the rhythm of your own soul flow through everything you do. And may your time gradually become the right time, every time you swing or dance.

YOUR STRENGTH

Fatigue comes in many forms, and as far as I can tell, it comes to all people, at all ages, in all areas of being alive. Yes, it can be seen simply as the bottom half of the sine wave, as energy ebbs and flows in foreseeable cycles of exertion and rest, day and night, summer and winter, youth and old age. But for most of us, fatigue strikes as an unwelcome aberration from any such routine. Simple rest does not replenish quite as well, relaxation does not rejuvenate as deeply, and spring does not return to the step as reliably as it once did.

Physical fatigue is a phenomenon that has been more studied than understood. Long-term sleep deprivation produces physiological effects that are baffling. A fellow college student stayed up all night two nights in a row studying for final exams, and the following day rode his bike full speed into a brick wall that he simply didn't see. A fellow officer volunteered for an Army experiment (don't ever do that) to see how long he could function without sleep. After 72 hours, surrounded by rotating shifts of dedicated soldiers whose sole duty was to keep him awake, he could no longer utter a coherent phrase, and later reported seeing a kaleidoscope of blue lights constantly before his eyes. Fatigue compromises function of every human faculty, and pushed to extremes, can do devastating or even fatal damage.

Mental fatigue is a different enemy altogether. Prolonged periods of intense concentration can produce not only severe headaches, but also a dense fog of disorientation that clouds perception, distorts decisions, and slows reactions. Driving while exhausted has long been understood to be as dangerous as driving while intoxicated. Decisions made at the end of a difficult work week tend to be less soundly reasoned than those made when well rested. In my software profession, I learned many years ago never to implement code changes on Friday afternoons; the risks of significant error were clearly higher than at any other time.

Most treacherous of all, from all I have seen and heard, is emotional fatigue. Prolonged sorrow, unresolved anger, unrelenting fear, persistent loneliness, and chronic anxiety can deplete the resources of the soul to devastating degrees. Even extended periods of overwhelming joy, intense gratitude, or enthusiastic expressions of purest love can also place unsustainable demands on your finite sources of energy and strength. Sometimes you need a vacation to recover from a wonderful vacation, or perhaps a little boredom scattered among your much-loved activity. Emotional rest is just as essential as the physical or mental varieties, yet somehow more elusive, and often less encouraged. How does one stop feeling, or even dampen the throbbing intensity of the most draining (or exhilarating) emotional experience?

Wait.

No, I don't mean wait for the answer... although that's not such a bad idea. I simply mean, "Wait." Defer. Delay. Procrastinate, on purpose. Whatever it is that seems urgent and pressing on your soul, don't act on it now. Don't respond to it yet. Don't react to it impulsively. Insert a pause into the pattern. Breathe, rest, count, and wait for the conductor's wand to bring you back into the music. Don't jump in early. Don't break the silence, don't interrupt the beautiful pause. Wait.

The rest in music is there for a reason. It gives the musician time to take a quick breath, to get ready for whatever comes next, or simply to relax as others take the lead. It is wise to rest, when opportunities appear. Don't just rest from your work; work from your rest. Don't think of rest as the something (or nothing) that you do after all your work is done; think of rest as an investment. Invest in rest ahead of time, to ensure your physical, mental, and emotional energy will sustain you through the work that lies ahead.

I often joke among my coworkers that the most difficult task I've ever been assigned is to do nothing. I'm not good at it, I don't excel at it, and I rarely succeed at it. The impulse to react, to fill the void, to do something even if it's wrong, too often overwhelms my resolve and prods me to do things better left undone, to say things better left unsaid, and to fix things that weren't really broken. The worst messes I've ever made came from jumping the gun, running out of my lane, and tinkering with things that were none of my business. Anticipation is my toughest foe, impatience my most troubling vice, and waiting my greatest challenge. But I do know that what I truly need to do much more often is, well... nothing.

Wait. Be still. Know that the world around you is not utterly dependent on you. Take the planet off of your shoulders and set it down for a while. If you need more visual reinforcement, try these three steps:

1) Place your hand in a bowl of water.
2) After 30 seconds, remove your hand.
3) Study the impression you made.

Stop. Wait. Be still. Understand that the world around you will continue to rotate, orbit, and function. It will soon enough be time to engage again in full activity and abundance.

But for now, for a moment or two, or maybe three, just wait. Your strength will be renewed. Count on it.

LEARN YOUR LIMITS

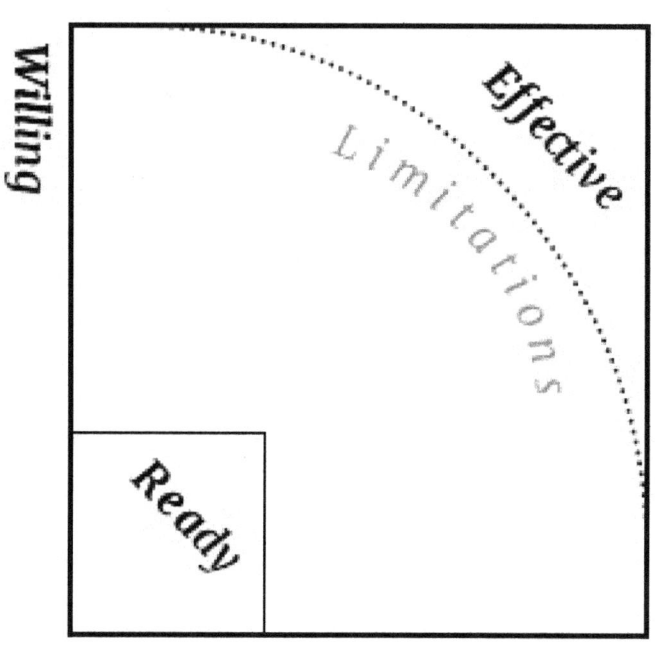

The human ear can typically discern sound waves in the range between 20 hertz (near the lowest pedal notes of a pipe organ) and 20,000 hertz. The highest note of a flute is at 2,093 hertz, the highest key of an 88-key piano resonates at 4,186 hertz. Dogs can apparently hear sounds up to 65,000 hertz. Elephants can hear frequencies as low as 14 hertz; whales as low as 7 hertz. Above or below our respective ranges, the "sound" waves are still there... we just can't hear them. We all have our limits, both in terms of what we can hear (or experience) and what we can say (or express). Learning to live within them, without despairing at our lack of ability, is very much a part of the experience of living, and of the practice of expression.

YOUR CAPABILITIES

On a good day, when my vocal cords are loose and lubricated (easy on the coffee), I can hit an E-flat without much strain, or an E, if I'm willing to risk the personal embarrassment of screeching and cracking a bit. On the low side, I can growl out a soft A without sounding too gravelly, but anything lower than that is just a muffled groan. That range puts me generally in the baritone section, if there is one. If not, I can hang out with the tenors until they reach for the upper deck, or with the basses until they dig under the crawl space.

The very low basses display a distinctive pride when they pass me on the way down the scale, knowing that I wish I could follow them into the depths. The tenors tend to be more focused on the challenge of their own task, knowing both the great risk and great reward of scaling uncommon heights. That puts my range at just over an octave and a half, a bit narrow for experienced vocalists, but sufficient to cover most popular hymns. Over time, I have learned my limits. I occasionally try to expand my range with practice (when I have the house to myself), but generally work within my zone of confidence.

On a good day, I can hike about seven miles up the moderate to strenuous trails of the Smoky Mountains, carrying a backpack with the necessary provisions. At that pace, I'm good for three or four days, before exhaustion overtakes enthusiasm. More accurately, that was my range about ten years ago, when backpacking was part of my annual rhythm. My capabilities have certainly diminished somewhat since then, and I would try something much less ambitious were I to venture out tomorrow. I have my limits, and I know that they change. They broaden with practice and general health, as they narrow with age and neglect.

On a good day, I am ready, willing, and able to meet all the expectations I have of myself, based on the very best of my own history and proven track record. On a very good day, I may well exceed those expectations, thus raising the expectations for the next very good day. On a bad day, I fail. Please don't try to tell me that I never fail. I can tell when my performance has not met my goals, as clearly as I can tell when a free throw does not go through the basketball net. Actually, I fail quite often — increasingly often as I increase the frequency and degree of difficulty of my attempts.

My good friend Chuck used to tell me that my biggest problem was that I had not yet failed enough. He attributed my readily apparent fear of failure to my simple lack of experience at failing. Most of what I attempted in my youth – at least in public — fell well within the range of things I knew I could do well. Whatever I wasn't good at I typically avoided, thus remaining contentedly incompetent in those arenas. The result was increasing confidence in a narrow range of activities, matched with increasing self-consciousness and anxiety in activities that lay outside that range. Due in large part to Chuck's encouragement and frequent chiding, I have in recent years made some modest gains in boldness. I now try more things that might not work, I attempt more things at which I do not excel, and I am more willing to reveal my lack of competence or mastery at various things (like golf) at which I hope to improve through practice.

On a very bad day, I simply fail to try. Not ready, not willing, not able, and thus not effective. Overly focused on the limitations that I know too well, I concede defeat before any effort is expended. I don't like those days. I don't like myself on those days. I don't like my limitations.

If I remember my theology lessons, it was the German theologian Emil Brunner who defined sin as a rejection of the truth of our limitations, a rebellion against the finite boundaries of our knowledge and power. We don't like being finite. It makes us feel weak, vulnerable, inadequate, and insecure. When I was younger, I could not grasp why the fruit of the Tree of Knowledge of Good and Evil would ever be forbidden. As I have aged, I have come to understand in small glimpses that the appeal of comprehensive understanding is a bit of a trap, as is the quest for unlimited power or unbounded fame. The beginning of wisdom may be said to reside in the understanding that we are not gods. We are not immortal, not omniscient, not omnipotent, and do not carry within us the potential to become any of those things. We live within finite yet flexible boundaries of what is possible, what is reasonable, and what is wise.

YOUR FRUSTRATIONS

There is an arrangement for classical guitar of J.S. Bach's "Jesu, Joy of Man's Desiring", credited to Joseph Castle, that I absolutely love. It is beautifully woven together, compelling in its seamless transitions, while demanding only a modest level of skill and technique — a level that is almost within my reach. Almost. I have practiced that piece for many hours on many different occasions over the span of four decades. To the best of my knowledge, I have played it correctly only once. Happily, that one time was at my brother's wedding. During the days and weeks leading up to that event, the hours of diligent repetition produced not only a disturbing thickness of calloused fingertips, but also noticeable decrease in the count of missed strings and misplaced fingers... enough to give me hope that I would not make an embarrassing mess of it when it truly counted. Whether due to divine intervention, a surge of adrenaline, or a combination of both, my fingers managed somehow to do what I asked of them, just that once.

I have attempted to replicate the feat in the privacy of my study countless times, with a handful of public renditions that were only mildly disappointing. (I prefer to play when I can provide merely background music, and avoid the attentive scrutiny of stage and lights.) I cannot explain exactly what it is that I have not been able to master, but as the 24th measure builds to the 25th, my fingers start tripping over each other like a team of wounded soldiers on a swinging bridge in a heavy storm. I've tried everything I know to try. I've slowed it down to the pace of a slothful snail. I have tried to piece it together one, two, or three notes at a time. I have played it faster, giving my hyperactive mind less time to think about what was coming next. Nothing has worked... at least not yet. I have not given up, and I don't believe I ever will. I tried again just a few minutes ago, and even as I write these words, I am trying to think of practice techniques that I may not have tried, or not tried enough.

It is, in a word, frustrating.

The frustration of a musician striving for perfection is no trivial matter, although it may certainly seem so, especially in contrast to matters of great practical or personal importance. Yet passionate musicians do not consider their craft in contrast to such matters, but rather embedded within them. To one devoted to the finest of arts, the expression of love is intertwined with love itself, and the expression of sorrow an essential element of grief. Life cannot be fully lived or experienced without also in some form being expressed. Thus, the fuming frustration of a musician is a poignant glimpse into the dramatic tensions that interfere in every aspect of our lives. If we cannot find words or means to express what we feel, then our feelings remain themselves in limbo, unresolved, maddeningly unsettled. When we cannot work through our most heartfelt declarations or most painful decisions without awkward ambiguities and painful misunderstandings, then the flow of energy is blocked, the urgent need for self-revelation deferred. Short of complete withdrawal from interaction with the world around us, we simply must work through the blockage, however many attempts it takes, to convey that which we intend to make clear, to reveal what we wish to make known.

We all want to be known, even as we anxiously fear the uncertain reactions to such knowledge. We desperately want to be loved as we truly are, and not as we might pretend to be. If we begin to feel chronically misunderstood, isolated in the uniqueness of our experience, unable to convey to anyone else the most urgent truths embraced by our very souls, then we become most hopelessly miserable, despondent, and at risk of losing our very desire to remain alive. These are not trivial matters. These are the things that simply must be learned, must be practiced, must be mastered, in order that we might fully become — and be known as — the people we truly are.

You will not master every phrase. Some particularly difficult passages simply need to be worked around. On one particularly strenuous trail in the Smoky Mountains, I plodded slowly around an uphill bend only to see the intimidating slope of yet another mountain peak immediately before me. Seeing my brief despair, my hiking partner called my attention to the fact that our trail led around that mountain, not over it. She added — out of strong insight into my tendencies — that not every mountain we see needs to be climbed. There are ways to get around intimidating obstacles, methods of navigating treacherous passages, innovative arrangements to overcome frightening difficulties. And yes, sometimes, you simply have to backtrack a bit, and find another trail. But none of these options constitute surrender. Quite the contrary, they capture the most creative aspects of the human soul. Find a way to say what needs to be said. Discover a new pathway to your passionate declaration. Blaze a new trail to your pinnacles of self-expression.

SECTION II: YOUR NOTES

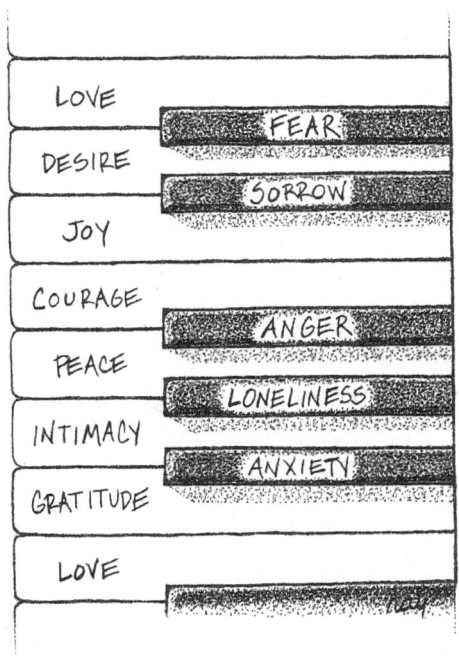

Within our uniqueness, we find elements of common experience. Within the limits of our range, we find instances where our expression resonates with the people around us, where we use the same words and the same phrases to voice the same truths. As distinctive as our melodies may be, we find connection and resonance in similar events, sympathetic reactions, and shared emotions. With perhaps infinite variations of tone, we nevertheless seem to know the same notes.

The best way I can think of to share what I know and feel about emotional expression is simply to share my own thoughts and emotional journeys with you. I am mindful that my own stories can provide you with little more than hints and suggestions — potential sparks to your own creative energy. I will tell stories of a dozen named emotions that I find to be quite common, and commonly wrestled with. In some cases, I will speak in the very present tense, as the events of my life inform and inspire my writing, even as the pages and paragraphs of this book are being written.

Rather than number these common emotions, I have chosen to associate them with the notes on a musical scale. They can be felt or shared or played in any order, in any combination, producing essentially limitless interactions and complex orchestrations. None of these emotions need be judged as good or bad, positive or negative, for all most certainly have their place in nearly every composition of any length. Nevertheless, I have chosen willfully to associate some emotions with the long keys of the piano, and others with the short keys. The reasons will be obvious, and the associations which you form with the notes themselves will likely be far beyond any that I could anticipate.

Rather than attempt to teach you how to express your feelings, I will simply express my own, preferably in ways that are reasonably transparent, in hopes that you may hear your own voice in some of my words.

A NOTE ABOUT NOTES

At the end of each section, you will find a page that looks something like this:

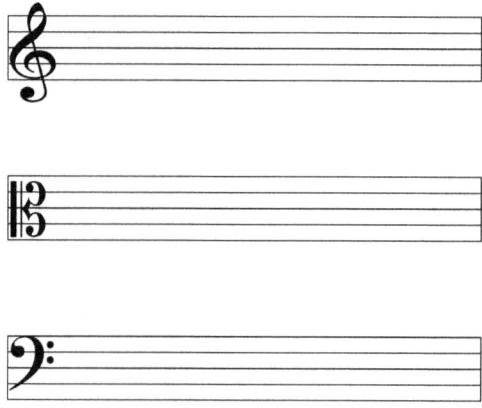

My intent is to encourage you to interact with what you have read, to write "notes" to yourself (electronically or mechanically), to engage in the practice of expressing your own thoughts and feelings about each topic as it is explored. The different staves are simply a reminder that there is a creative, artistic, and in some respect musical quality to everything we express. Use them, if at all, in whatever way suits you. Ask yourself a question, leave yourself a reminder, or compose a line of your next symphony. They are, after all, your notes.

C – CONFESSING LOVE

> *If I speak with the tongues of men and of angels,*
> *But do not have love,*
> *I have become a noisy gong or a clanging cymbal.*
> *(1 Corinthians 13:1, New American Standard Bible)*

Despite its position at the root of all human emotion and the center of human experience, love can be surprisingly tricky to express, particularly when it is felt most deeply, and the longing to express it clamors most urgently.

It hit me when I was in fourth grade. Her name was Melanie. She was cute, bright, and spunky, and everything she said or did held my attention as a willing captive. I was mesmerized by her, to the point of losing track of whatever else was going on around me. The feeling inside of me — whatever name you wish to give it — was pleading with my wobbly, distracted mind to give it a voice, to proclaim its presence, and confess its truth. I wanted to tell her what I was feeling, but I was extraordinarily unsure of how she would react, completely clueless about how to approach the revelation, and paralyzed by the potential implications of all that might or might not follow.

It seems there is no true way to express your love for another person without exposing yourself to the vulnerable trepidation of not knowing how the other person will respond. Love is by its very nature a shared emotion, and the very possibility that it might be felt by one and not the other is unnerving to contemplate. The expression of love is essentially and necessarily an invitation to love back. In order to be fully received, love must also be given, and in order for the gift to be fulfilled, it must be willingly received. Love that is rejected never becomes what it wanted to be, and love that is ignored is merely a fleeting spark that never found the fuel to become a fire.

So we hesitate. We hide. We camouflage our feelings out of self-preservation, ducking for cover before any real threat of rejection has a chance to appear. We substitute like for love, and settle for comfortable companionship, rather than risk the rib-rending exposure of an open and vulnerable heart... unless we are foolish... or fearless... or perhaps a bit of both.

I torqued what little courage I could reach, and at the next random opportunity — while passing briefly in the hallway — I blurted out quickly and awkwardly the only words that had any claim on the truth of that moment: "I love you!" It didn't go well. She turned abruptly into the girls' restroom, with a look of shock and dismay on her face that I cannot forget. I don't believe she spoke to me for days, maybe weeks. My wiser, calmer, cooler friend Mike tried to help, to point out a few of the many things I had done terribly wrong, and nudge me gently in the direction of a more artful and gracious mode of self-expression. Mike was a good friend, especially in that moment, but in me he had very little to work with, and he did not have enough time to teach me what he somehow already knew.

(Melanie — if you ever read this, please accept my deepest apology for my inept clumsiness and complete lack of grace or charm. I can only imagine the awkwardness and embarrassment I caused you, even if only for that moment. I still think of you as the most wonderful girl I met in grade school, and I am grateful for what my heart learned from knowing you.)

It is risky to love at all, and all the more risky to express that love. We might not ever do it at all, were it not for that mysterious, overpowering hope that we might also be loved. And we might not have that hope, were it not for some deep sensation of unseen trust, perhaps from having been loved before we can remember, perhaps from knowing the love of those who raised or conceived us, or of the one who created us. This is a mystery that I cannot unlock, and yet, like all who have lived before me and all who will live beyond, I have learned ways to express it, to show it, to share it. With years of practice and perseverance — and lessons learned from legions of blunders — I dare say that I am better at it than I was before. Mastered it, I have not. But I find that at least I am less afraid to say "I love you", when those words capture the truth arising from my soul. And I have become deeply committed to continuing to speak those words, and to express their truth, in as many different ways as I can imagine.

Notes about Love

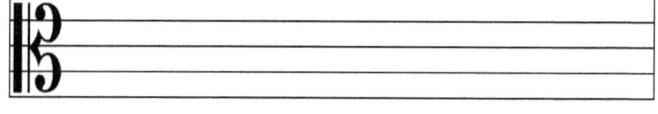
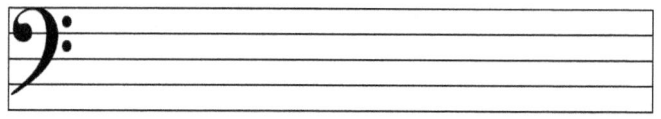

C# – THE POINT OF FEAR

> *The Lord is my light and my salvation;*
> *Whom shall I fear?*
> *The Lord is the defense of my life;*
> *Whom shall I dread?*
> *(Psalm 27:1, NASB)*

Fear will be expressed, whether you wish it so or not. Fear is most likely to express itself in action, rather than words, although a variety of involuntary expletives and guttural vocalizations may be involved. You might scream or squeal; you might cuss or cry; you might groan, gasp, or whimper. You may run for the hills or turn and face your attacker. There is even a chance you will freeze in place, in petrified indecision — but even that would be but a brief deferral, with action to follow briskly whenever wits allow.

Action is the point of fear. We are designed to react to danger, with adrenaline rushing to fuel either flight or fight, and all sensors on full alert, gathering data for immediate use and deferred contemplation.

Even the simplest retreat of a burned fingertip from a hot stove is powerful evidence of the speed of our self-preservation. We will seek survival — either our own or that of those we love — in every circumstance, and only wisdom and experience can teach us which threats are less dangerous than they appear.

It was either a collie or a German shepherd (my memory is fuzzy on that detail). It seemed friendly enough at first, walking up to us in a wooded lot near our home, where we liked to play. I was a bit more trusting than my older brother (he would say naive, foolish, or perhaps stupid). I wanted to greet the canine neighbor, as gently and kindly as I knew how. It was not a good idea. The appearance of benevolence vanished in the blink of an eye, replaced with exposed cuspids and incisors clearly intent on inspiring fear. Inspire they did, for my next remembered thought was one of anxious gratitude for the less-than-gentle boost my brother provided as we scampered up a familiar tree, urged on by angry growls and menacing barks.

We were in that tree for quite a while. Various escapes were attempted, when our warden seemed distracted or disinterested. Each attempt was met with fierce resistance and loud rebuke. As the failures mounted, and the day grew long, the intense energy of survival faded into a heavy sense of dread. Yes, of course, we had yelled for help. No one heard, or no one came. I was afraid.

It is written that the fear of the Lord is the beginning of wisdom. Surely wisdom must begin with an understanding that there are things in this world more powerful than ourselves, and that all of our efforts to master our own fate serve only to illustrate our weakness and accentuate our ineptitude. Of all the powers to be feared, it seems only fitting that our greatest fears would be focused on the greatest powers, and that our primary fear should be centered on the source of all power. We can only hope that the one who holds the greatest power does not intend to harm us, but rather (dare we be so bold as to hope this?) that he intends good for us, and would bring us help in our time of need.

At one point I remembered that Papaw was coming over that evening. Dad was out of town (as he often was), and a visit from Papaw was a special treat. We were supposed to be home by now, judging from the distance between the sun and the ridge. Mom would surely come looking for us. She might be angry that we were late for dinner, but at least she would come.

My heart leapt when I saw Papaw's distinctive black Oldsmobile drive by on the road, a hundred yards or so away, heading to our house. Within minutes we heard Mom's voice, calling us home, and then she heard ours. With an abbreviated shout of encouragement, she went to get her father.

It seemed only seconds until the black Oldsmobile reappeared, this time heading towards us. The tall, stern figure of my grandfather unfolded from the driver's seat, grasping firmly to a log as thick as my head, plucked from the woodpile beside the back door. I cannot explain how, but I do believe the dog knew at that moment exactly what we knew: that Papaw was bigger, stronger, and — if necessary — meaner than the dog. Papaw held the power, and the dog was now the one retreating in fear. We were safe.

Franklin Roosevelt once taught us that we have nothing to fear but fear itself. I believe that in that timeless line, he showed a deep understanding: that fear serves a useful yet temporary purpose. We need to experience fear, to act on fear, to learn from fear... but we need not remain in fear. Fear needs — no, demands — to be resolved. Safety must be sought, with all the resolve we can muster, until it is found; it must be asked for until it is given; its door must be beat upon until it is opened.

When fear strikes, by all means act! Run, yell, climb, swim, fight! Don't bother worrying about who might think you weak for showing your fear. Fear comes to us all. Express it with all your might. Sound the alarm. Give it full voice. And when your might is not enough, and your voice grows hoarse from calling out, cling to that one wondrous hope: that your voice will be heard, that you indeed will be rescued by one more powerful than all your enemies, who brings you help when you need it most.

Then, and only then... don't be afraid.

Notes about Fear

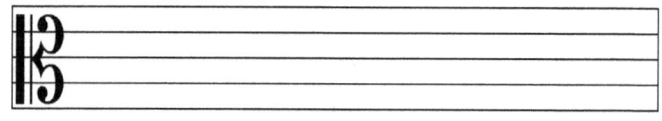

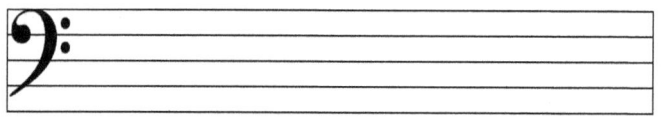

D – DARING TO DESIRE

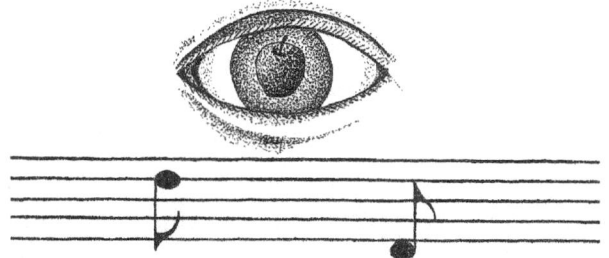

> *Trust in the Lord and do good;*
> *Dwell in the land and cultivate faithfulness.*
> *Delight yourself in the Lord;*
> *And He will give you the desires of your heart.*
> *(Psalm 37:3-4, NASB)*

What do you want? Emphasize each different word, and you get four different tones. Vary the pitch and length of each syllable, and the meanings multiply even more. Desire has a big range. We have a lot of ways of wanting.

We need. We wish. We hope.
We ask. We seek. We knock.
We hunger. We thirst. We reach.
We dream. We envision. We pursue.

I desire my wife. I will be discreet, but this is no reason for me to be ashamed. There are no fig leaves required here. She is bright and beautiful, alluring and elusive, engaging and perplexing, captivating and freeing. She conceals and reveals, she shares and withholds, she approaches and withdraws. She stimulates my desire to be with her, to know her and be known by her, to connect with her in every chord of mind, body and spirit.

Desire is dangerous. Let there be no doubt about that. If you find that one special pearl of great value, you may find yourself selling everything you have so that you can buy it. This is not necessarily rational behavior; but the heart has its reasons that reason does not know (as Pascal so pointedly proclaimed). We are driven by forces we do not understand, guided by impulses we cannot explain, and infused with passions that overwhelm our senses. This can be frightening, both to those caught up in the whirlwind and to those contemplating whether and how to avoid it. It can change everything.

No, not every desire is pure. Most of them aren't, to be honest. Most guitars are out of tune, most portraits are hanging crooked, and most arrows miss the bullseye. The air we breathe, the water we drink, and the thoughts that we ponder all have impurities and toxins that must be dealt with — unless you decide to stop breathing, drinking, or thinking. Our minds and bodies have impressive organic functions and redundancies to process much of the toxicity that comes our way, but that doesn't mitigate the need for caution and circumspection. It's never a good idea to drink downstream from the herd.

We have a universal and natural need to purify our own desires. Wisdom and maturity are measured in large part by our capacity to cultivate our most noble desires, at the expense of their lesser rivals. And this process of growth transforms the desires themselves. Eating nothing but candy and sweets all day sounded wonderful, until I did it. After the consequences were understood, it didn't sound so good anymore. But wisdom comes slowly, if at all, and not every hangover inspires future moderation. Generally speaking, we need help with the process of growing up, of understanding what good really looks like, and of recognizing which desires are most worthy of pursuit.

This is the fundamental challenge of desire. The ascetics would say we shouldn't permit ourselves any desires, for they are unpredictable and powerful and so often lead to situations far beyond our control. The authoritarians would say that our desires are offensive, and indicate a lack of gratitude for all the wonderful things we already have. The despondent and the melancholy would find our desires fanciful and insubstantial — charging at windmills, so to speak — serving only to distract us from the mundane demands of our necessary existence.

To all these voices of dissonance, I would simply say, "Silence!" (or as my wife would say, "Sit down somewhere!") The most celebrated King of Israel — the one who danced naked in the streets, who was captivated by the beauty of Bathsheba, who deeply desired and did many very wonderful and not so wonderful things — this is the David who was fully alive, and grandly depicted by Michelangelo with fig leaf removed. This was the same David who wrote and sang the timeless songs of faith and despair to the Lord, whom he both greatly loved and greatly feared.

This is the David who is known as the man after God's own heart.

I pursued my wife. She says that she pursued me. Whichever one is most correct, I know this most certainly: my heart has never been fuller or more fully alive than when I am in her company. I adore her; I cherish her; I pursue her; I enjoy her. And I thank God every day for allowing our paths to cross, for giving us each eyes to behold the wonder in the other, for giving us the strength and courage to seek out the other, and for ultimately granting me the deepest desire of my heart.

Allow me to exhort you: dare to know your own deepest desires. Learn them, cultivate them, filter them, prune them, purify them, and celebrate them. Seek and receive help in recognizing those most worthy of wholehearted pursuit. Then, pursue them, for all you're worth. Don't be afraid, don't hold back, and don't look back. The Lord may indeed grant you your heart's deepest desires. And surely, goodness and mercy will follow you all the days of your life. And you will dwell in the house of the Lord forever.

Notes about Desire

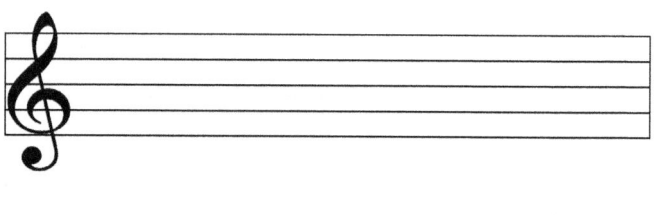

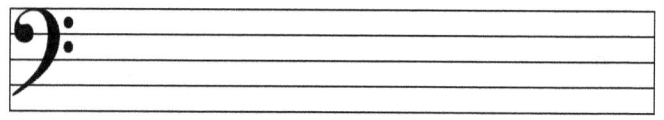

D# – THE SHADOW OF SORROW

> *Even though I walk through the valley of the shadow of death,*
> *I fear no evil, for You are with me;*
> *Your rod and Your staff, they comfort me.*
> *(Psalm 23:4, NASB)*

How do you describe what isn't there? That shape on the ground where the light can't reach, because its path is blocked by a tree or a mountain or a bird: we call it a shadow, but it is hardly a thing at all. It is simply an absence of light, taking on the distinctive distorted appearance of whatever blocks the light, and somehow taking on more meaning in its emptiness than all the light diffused around its odd silhouette.

The light dancing off the surface of the lake gives the striking impression of things in or on the water that simply aren't there. The colorful fall leaves, the brilliant white clouds, the unknown depths of clear blue sky cannot be contained in or by the lake itself; they can't really be there at all. They are elsewhere, not even in that direction really, yet close enough and recent enough to still be noticed, even where they aren't. The light which couldn't reach the shadow found its way to the lake, and from the surface of the lake to me, to tell me fanciful tales and magical memories of things at once near and far.

When a stranger suggests that you turn left where the big old oak used to be, there is trust that you knew the oak, and know the place where it was, known mostly by locals precisely because of the former dominating presence of the old oak tree that was there. The oak isn't there now, but the place still is, and it is still known that way: for what was there once, but isn't now, except in the sense that the place still bears its presence, as it bears its absence. If you didn't know the oak, then you probably didn't know the people whose initials were once carved in its trunk, nor the man who as a boy broke his left arm trying to climb to the top. You wouldn't remember the ample shade it offered on hot summer days, or the symphony that played in its branches when strong winds passed through. If you missed knowing the oak, you'll probably miss that left turn too, for you cannot recognize the significance of the place where it used to be.

Chuck isn't here anymore.

Could it have been fifteen years already? It still hurts to write those words. And it frightens me a bit to continue writing... for I don't know how dark this shadow is nor how deep this lake may be, should I be bold enough to approach and examine what I already know is no longer there. If I start, I may not be able to stop. If I speak, my own ears will suffer the sound and sense of my words. If I share my thoughts, then my thoughts will be unleashed, and unconstrained. My thoughts cannot undo the loss, but I am at a loss to know what such thoughts might yet do. Like shadows on a hill, reflections on a lake, or oak trees that provide direction long after they're gone, such thoughts may do something that I cannot fully understand. They may resonate with your thoughts, and yours with mine.

Charles Tobias Sikler was my best friend. He was my business partner. We went to seminary together. We went to church together. We raised our children together. We sought marital advice from each other, and we each seemed to understand the other's wife better than our own. After seminary, when we lived in different towns, we would call each other on a Saturday night to work through what we were preaching the next morning. We took very long walks together, to accommodate even longer conversations. We debated every topic of theology, politics, and culture. We pointed out each other's weaknesses, and rather boldly suggested corrective actions. No one else could have gotten away with that, but the other one of us.

We weren't very much alike, really. He was bold and bombastic; I was understated and socially cautious. He was larger than life with a vast colorful background, I was known mostly for my potential, seeking courage to venture out and try my wings. He was Jewish by birth, and had his Bar Mitzvah in Haifa, Israel. He became a Christian as a seasoned adult. I was raised in a Protestant home, and came to faith at a Billy Graham

Crusade in Knoxville when I was 10. He was a fundamentalist, and I was a moderate — at a time when fundamentalists and moderates were fighting for control of the seminary and the denomination. We disagreed about almost every topic that came up... sometimes just for sport, but often from deep-seated convictions not easily relinquished. He was unorthodox in all his manner, but traditional in his beliefs; I was contrarian in my philosophy, but speciously compliant in my conduct. He would stir things up; I would calm things down. I wanted to be more like him, and he more like me... but in a limited sense, for each of us.

His background was rough, and he bore many scars from it. His father had survived a Russian prison camp in the Holocaust. His parents divorced, and fought an ugly custody battle... each trying to force the other to take custody, neither wanting it. His mother remarried, but ended up killing his abusive stepfather, and went to prison for it. Chuck ended up making his own way, and getting quite lost in the process. A drug addict living on the streets of Seattle in the turbulence of the 1960s, he was rescued from critical illness by a compassion prostitute who roamed the same streets. He came to faith in a bar, through the patient persistence of a local pastor, and by way of a sudden realization that none of his bar friends would likely go out of their way to attend his funeral.

His past always impacted his present. An XXL personality was housed in an XXL body, and drugs and indulgences had taken a toll on how well that body could function. A surgery to do critical repair resulted in relentless infection. He was in a coma for months, but emerged from it, and slowly returned to as close to normal as he could get. Health problems continued, and shortly before he turned 50, another surgery was attempted. He did not leave that hospital alive.

I cannot and would not forget the day that his wife, Carol, called, facing a horrible decision. The team of doctors had gathered, confronting the faint threads of hope that they had pursued as far as they could, and brought their compassionate cruel recommendation to Carol. Carol called me to ask not what I thought she should do, but what Chuck would want her to do. She knew that I knew Chuck's heart better than I knew my own. Yes, I knew without any shadow or reflection of doubt exactly what he would want. It was not at all what I wanted. Like I said, we hardly ever agreed about anything. But brilliant rays of light streamed through branches of old trees at just that moment, illuminating the place where I was with a clarity that I had never seen before, and I boldly and tearfully told Carol what I knew, and what I know that she knew as well.

And after I had said what I deeply didn't want to say, it occurred to me to ask whether anyone had asked Chuck what he wanted. It was an odd question, really. Chuck had hardly been awake at all for many weeks, and when he was awake he wasn't coherent, and he didn't make sense. And that wasn't Chuck... because for as long as I knew him, even when I knew he was wrong, he always made sense.

But that day was different. He was awake. He was thinking. He was curious. He was Chuck. By the time Carol built up the unthinkable courage to ask him the unspeakable question, Chuck had already asked it himself. Just before Carol had entered the room, Chuck had asked the nurse what would happen if that sophisticated machine by his bed were turned off. He knew the answer. His was a brilliant, restless mind, and part of his storied past included a few years as an EMT, a respiratory specialist at that. He knew what would happen. And he knew what he wanted. Carol gave voice to the question; Chuck gave voice to the answer: "I need you to let me go." I will never know the pain that she endured in giving honor to that impossible request.

The hospital was about a three-hour drive from where I was. By the time I got there, all the decisions had been made... well, almost all of them. As I walked into his room, the nurse was asking if there was anything he would like to eat or drink. All the dietary restrictions were lifted. He was free to choose. "Caffeine-Free Diet Coke", was his answer. Perhaps I was too accustomed to challenging his every thought. "Really, Chuck? Diet?? You know you can have the real stuff if you want it now, right?" He assured me that he had stated his preference; he liked the taste of it better. Like I said, he knew what he wanted.

He also knew what he wanted for his funeral. Of course he asked me to do it. No, that's not right. He instructed me to do it. He instructed me on how to do it, whom to involve, what scriptures and hymns to include. At that point, it really didn't matter anymore what I wanted. Not that it didn't matter to him: it didn't matter to me. The only thing I cared about in those moments was what Chuck wanted, what he desired most deeply, what he longed and hungered and thirsted for. I cared only about that, because I loved him.

Perhaps the nurse thought it would help me, or him, or both of us. The nurse gently invited me to stay in the room while the machines were shut down. I couldn't, but I did. I can't explain how. He even asked me to turn off a machine... assuring me it wasn't yet the final machine. I did. And I said goodbye. And so did Chuck. And I left the room with tears streaming down my cheeks, much as they are beginning to stream again now.

Chuck's not here anymore. He died on Passover. Visitation was on Good Friday. The funeral was the day after Easter. A host of angels was in attendance, singing in full voice all the hymns he had picked out. I opened with Shema Yisrael, "Hear O Israel, the Lord our God, the Lord is One", in the best Hebrew I could muster. The key hymn was "Victory in Jesus". Four preachers who knew and loved him spoke, each selected by Chuck, and each a dear friend of his, including me. None of us could have managed it alone.

The last scripture was Romans 1:16, "I am not ashamed of the gospel, for it is the power of God that brings salvation to everyone who believes: first to the Jew, then to the Gentile." They carried out the casket while we lifted our voices to the heavens, singing Darlene Zschech's "Shout to the Lord". The resonance of that moment within my soul has never diminished.

Chuck is not here anymore, and I miss him very much, very often. Yet his absence is here — profoundly and poignantly here — and that matters... a lot.

Notes about Sorrow

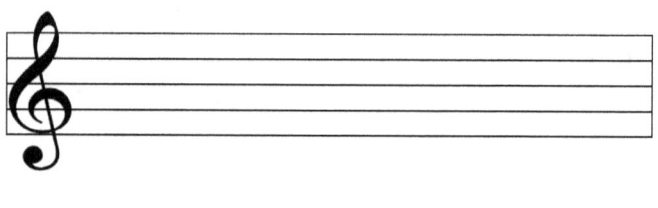

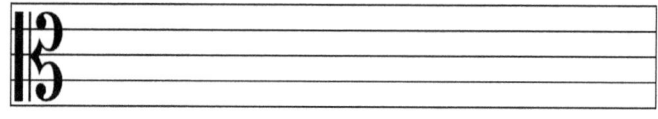

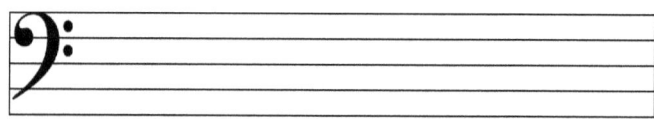

E – ENTERING INTO JOY

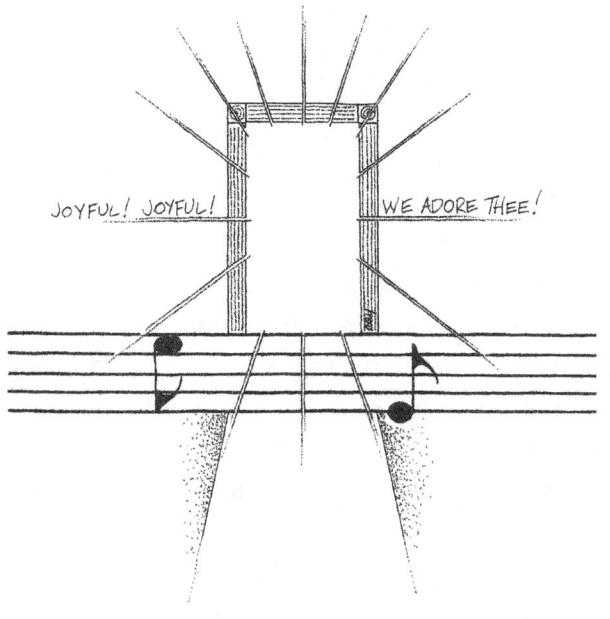

> *You will make known to me the path of life;*
> *In Your presence is fullness of joy;*
> *In Your right hand there are pleasures forever.*
> *(Psalm 16:11, NASB)*

I have heard it said in sundry ways that happiness comes to you, while joy comes through you. We see ourselves quite often as recipients of life's events, rather than participants in them. We function as audience more readily than as actors; we observe our surroundings when we might be shaping them; we pay attention to trends and tendencies, while opportunities to lead and guide pass too frequently unnoticed and untaken.

I had an opportunity to direct a choir once. I almost missed it. But before I tell you about that choir, I need to tell you about the woman who gave birth to it: Alice.

Alice was one of the first people that I met and got to know in Bloomfield, the wondrously small town in Kentucky where I began my journey as a pastor. Alice was the organist for the church — I should say churches, for they were a Presbyterian and a Baptist church meeting and worshipping together, sharing everything except a name and a bank account. Alice was a Methodist, but the Presbyterian-Baptist church had needed an organist, and she had taken the opportunity gladly, denomination notwithstanding.

How many years she had been there, I do not know, but she most certainly belonged there. Her gifts and her spirit filled the sanctuary in more ways than one. The church itself — the Presbyterian side — had been around for nearly 200 years before I got there; the Baptists had been with them about 15 years. Their ability to work and worship together was remarkable, and a central part of their identity. Alice was a big part of making it work. She brought people together, in everything she did.

After my first sermon there — just filling in for a friend — Alice invited me to her house for lunch. Her husband, Paul Ray, joined in the invitation, but to be honest, Alice almost always did all the talking. The invitation was accepted, and I began to meet and get to know her family... a vast and complex undertaking that took a good 20 years, and continues even to this day. She also introduced me to Scott Kilgore, the pastor of the Disciples of Christ church in town, who happened to drop by just after lunch. They were good friends, and I came to understand that Alice was pretty much a good friend to every church and community leader in the county, and in most of the neighboring counties.

One of Alice's many projects — and perhaps the one nearest to her heart and soul — was the community choir. She and Leland Parks, the music minister from the larger Baptist church in town, had shared a vision for pulling choirs together from all around to sing in a living Christmas tree, which they named the Tree of

Life. They pulled it off, marvelously and gloriously. It became the main event of Advent. Singers came from twenty or thirty different churches throughout the region, and rehearsed every week from Labor Day to Thanksgiving. Then pretty much the whole town pitched in to build the immense structure, to hold the 60 or 70 singers, along with more lights and decorations than anyone could count. They set it up in the Methodist church, because they had the highest ceiling. The Tree fit the sanctuary beautifully, as if designed for each other. By the time I came along, they were doing 16 presentations every year, between Thanksgiving and Christmas, filling up the sanctuary with over 200 enthusiastic listeners and worshippers for each and every one. They charged a dollar per ticket, just to keep track of how many they could seat, and to help offset the costs. There weren't a lot of costs; almost everything needed was volunteered and donated. Whatever was left over each year went to local charities.

It was a wonderful thing, this Tree of Life.

... to be continued...

JOY, INTERRUPTED

I got stuck right here, while writing. For a couple of weeks, I couldn't find my way forward in my own thoughts. I wasn't even sure how to put into words why I was stuck. The words trying to form in my head just didn't sound right; they didn't match my feelings; they didn't ring true in my soul.

On a whim, I called one of Alice's daughters, who had recently reconnected with me. (She and her husband moved back to Kentucky a few months ago, and bought a house just across the highway from us. We're neighbors now.)

I told her about this book that I am writing — or trying to write — and about the significance of her mother in the current chapter. Her reaction surprised me, because my story surprised her. It seems that she and I experienced the same events from vastly different perspectives. What was to me a story of great joy came from a period of great tension. She was not aware of the joy I had witnessed, as I was not aware of the struggle she had endured. We had walked alongside the same people through the same events, but we had not seen or heard the same things. We had not shared our thoughts with each other, until now.

Talking with Alice's daughter did not get me unstuck in my writing. It got me more stuck, mired more deeply in mud I couldn't move. Something was wrong with the way I was thinking about joy. It wasn't until today that I began to understand what was blocking my view, and suppressing the flow of creative thought. There was a dissonance in my recollection. A duet of discordant reactions pulled my thoughts in different directions, and I couldn't seem to focus on one without the other.

And the tension was coming from the remembrance of the story itself. It wasn't just Alice's daughter who felt deep pain through those events, although she likely felt its suffocating grip as profoundly as anyone. The whole community knew the long, hard struggle that Alice and her family faced. Alice fought a long and frustrating fight with cancer. There were surgeries, and treatments, and dramatic changes in behavior and family dynamics. There were awkward shifts from despair to hope, and back to despair. I certainly knew the pain second-hand; I was her pastor, and she confided in me with great clarity and conviction. But I also knew it first-hand. I hurt with her, and for her, and I really hated what was happening to her. Her loss was a rough, rugged, gut-wrenching loss to the community, to the churches, to her large and complex family, and also to me. But that's not the part of the story I wanted to tell. It's not the part I wanted to remember.

I simply couldn't get to the telling of the joy without also wrestling with the pain, no matter how much I would rather focus on the former and forget the telling of the latter. But it doesn't work that way. You can't get there from here, as they say, at least not without going through the parts you'd rather go around. So I shall proceed with the telling of the story — but only because I can now admit and acknowledge the tension that is in it, the discordant emotions that ought not to occupy the same space at the same time, yet do.

Maybe it is true that without darkness we could not comprehend light, nor without sadness could we ever enter into joy.

It was an amazing thing, this Tree of Life.

ENTERING INTO JOY (CONTINUED)

They asked me to lead it, after Leland moved away. I had no particular qualifications; playing banjo and guitar hardly qualifies one for leading and directing the most passionate, talented and diverse assemblage of dedicated singers and musicians in the region. Yet those that asked me let me know that they needed my heart, a pastor's heart, to hold together a flock that was showing signs of splintering after their shepherd, Leland, had left.

I agonized over the decision. The level of commitment of time, energy, and concern was clearly deeper than any I had ever taken on before. The standards were high, the tradition now significant, and the symbolic power throughout the larger community undeniable. I knew that I must say "yes" before I even contemplated the question, yet contemplate I did, in the foundations of my soul.

I said "yes" for Alice. She wasn't the one who asked me, but I knew what she wanted me to do, and I knew she had more confidence in me than I had in myself. I also knew, in ways I cannot explain, that the journey was one that I needed to take.

For the next seven years, my calendar, my energy, and my passion were both dominated and empowered by the mission which was the Tree of Life. Every degree of anxiety, awe, frustration, fulfilment, fatigue, gratitude, and hope that I had ever experienced was exceeded in the annual rhythm of inspiration, preparation, adaptation, and unfettered worship. Surrounded by an extended community that fought and bickered like siblings, yet worked together and harmonized like a host of divine messengers, I had without question the best seat in the house. When it all came together, as it always somehow did, the force of beauty that emerged overwhelmed my hearing and stirred my very soul, filling my being with an unquenchable joy that endures to this day. The celebration of Christmas will be for me always linked to the glorious opportunity to be a part of this choir, to play my part in its drama, to lend my heart to its purpose. My arms still move in directing motions at the sound and even the memory of those beautiful hymns and choral arrangements — although I never truly felt that I was directing the music, but rather that the music and the worship were directing me. I was simply allowing them to overwhelm me, to fill me, to find their full expression in every part of me.

There is another connection to that Tree of Life that for me shall never die. Alice's long fight with cancer ended one December day, while final preparations for that year's Tree of Life were being made. It was beyond appropriate; it was necessary that the memorial service for Alice be conducted there, in the sanctuary of the Methodist church, at the center, root, and foundation of that substantial tree. Leland returned for the service, and he and I officiated. Many others spoke, and shared, and cried — giving voice to countless stories and preservatives to memories that must be treasured. It would fall to me to find final words to be spoken, yet such words I could not find. Instead, the words found me:

"Well done, good and faithful servant. Enter now into the joy of your Lord."

Notes about Joy

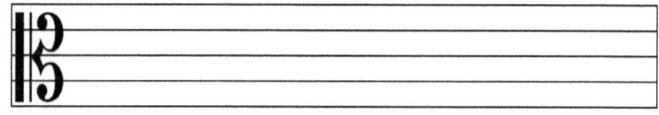

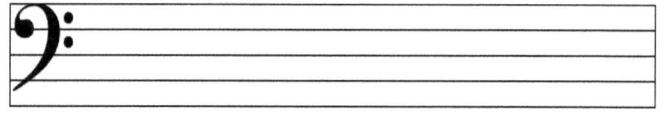

F – FINDING COURAGE

> *Have I not commanded you?*
> *Be strong and courageous!*
> *Do not tremble or be dismayed,*
> *For the Lord your God is with you wherever you go.*
> *(Joshua 1:9, NASB)*

Courage is invisible. It tends also to be quiet: a pianissimo persistence of patient passion that flows like an underground stream, pushing steadily through impediments of solid granite.

Courage is not the absence of fear, just as love is not the absence of hate nor joy the absence of sorrow. Rather, courage rises to the surface when summoned by fear, when urgency demands action yet caution blocks the clarity of will.

There is no time to cultivate courage once it is needed, no time to search for it when the danger is at hand. Courage must simply exist in a state of quiet readiness, like second-string quarterbacks and Broadway understudies who never quite know when or whether their services may be required. It must be prepared, trained, and alert at all times, standing watch at the gates of the seemingly peaceful fortress.

I need courage now. Today my father was released from the hospital, with a blood clot in his heart and several in his lungs. He is officially in no immediate danger, yet considered at very high risk of a life-ending event — and I cannot wrap my head around how both of those statements can possibly be true at the same time. His heart is weak, operating at roughly 20% of its capacity and need. He will sleep most of the time, to conserve what little strength he has. He is at home, with my mother and his wife of over 60 years, and with a caring and wonderful CNA, taking her regular shift at watching over them, helping them in any way they need.

My father has dementia, which has been progressing for perhaps ten years. I cannot tell now what he knows or what he is thinking. He smiles a lot, and seems much more relaxed and content than he did when the demands of work and family required his peak performance, which was always practically indistinguishable from perfection.

When he was head of operations at the Air National Guard base in Knoxville, a banner hung above the headquarters entrance which proclaimed and demanded "Zero Defects", which I felt described quite aptly both the character and the expectations of my father. It was among my jobs as a young boy to set the table for dinner, served always promptly at 6pm (or 1800 hours, for those who spoke his language). The table was to be set in accordance with the published rules of Amy Vanderbilt's etiquette, with one notable exception: there was no need to place a napkin beside my father's plate, for he did not make mistakes, and never spilled anything. Ever.

They moved from California to North Carolina about seven years ago, to be closer to family members that were scattered throughout the region. They now live about a six-hour drive from our home in Kentucky, and we are able to see them more often. At our last visit, about a month ago, my father was smiling even more than usual. He said many things to me, with affection and patience in his voice, but the pattern of words did not form any meaningful phrase that I could discern... until it was time to leave. Then he slowly stood and approached, placed a gentle hand on my shoulder, rocked his bent finger in pleasant contemplation, with a caring laugh in his tone and a brilliant twinkle in his deep-set blue eyes, and said clearly and simply, "You remind me of someone." If my simple presence still brings associations of affection and happiness to the labyrinth of my father's weakened mind, then that is something for me to keep and treasure for as long as I have breath.

I need courage now, for danger seems near, and fog clouds my judgement. I don't know what is coming next, or when, but I know it shall be something that I have not faced before, certainly not of this magnitude or force. Yesterday, for the first time in my life, my mother was ready and willing to share with me their thoughts and feelings about final arrangements. No, I was not at all prepared for that; yet my lack of preparation was at that point irrelevant. A simple graveside service was all, with just immediate family. I suggested a small memorial service near the assisted living community that is now their home, so the people there could say their goodbyes. I asked about the gravesite, and she did not know. I suggested Arlington, where his brother John was interred about three years ago. Mom's first reaction was that they did not deserve Arlington. I corrected her. He does, and they do. When we had the same conversation again about 20 minutes later, she liked the idea of Arlington very much, if I could make the arrangements, and take her there. I assured her that I could and would.

I was in no way ready for that conversation. Nor was I prepared for the conversation with the kind lady from Palliative Care, who gently and compassionately explained the availability of Hospice Care. I thought that conversation was still a ways away, over the horizon. It wasn't; it is here, now, whether or not I am ready.

It is time for me to sleep now, and conserve the strength that I have left. Tomorrow (technically, later today) is a new day, with new dangers and new decisions. I hope that my courage will be ready when I need it. Right now, I can neither see nor hear it. Yet perhaps it is there, flowing beneath the surface, gaining strength from all that has come before, and from an underground network of brooks and streams that connect all of creation with sustaining power.

Notes about Courage

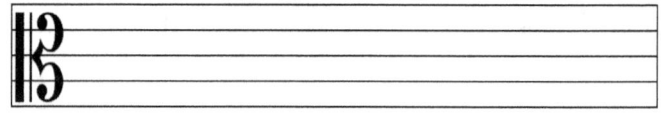

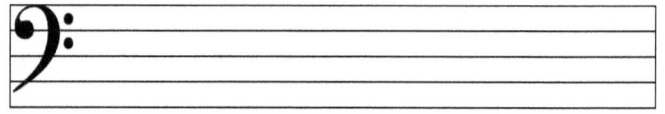

F# – THE SPEED OF ANGER

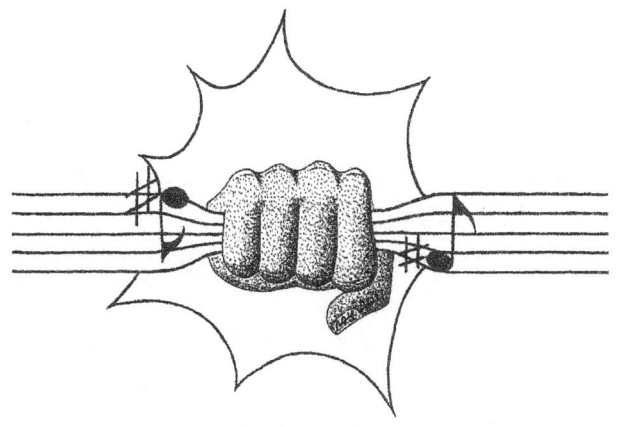

> *He who is slow to anger*
> *Is better than the mighty,*
> *And he who rules his spirit,*
> *Than he who captures a city.*
> *(Proverbs 16:32, NASB)*

I don't remember hitting him. In fact, I didn't remember hitting him even right after I apparently did, and I have never had any recollection of the angry outburst itself, only of the events immediately before and after. It just happened too fast.

I think I must have been 13, just after the end of eighth grade. My older brother was annoying me, which is sort of like saying the sun had risen that morning. This time he crossed a line, one that neither of us had ever seen or anticipated. His transgression was surely minor; he never did actual harm. He caused me pain often, physical damage never: I'm not sure how he kept those boundaries clear, but he always did. On that occasion, I did not. By the time Mom came into the room, I was holding a bicycle pump, and my brother was holding his head. The obvious question must have been rhetorical, for the answer to "What happened?!?" was radically obvious to all present.

From what I remember of my Army training in explosives, there are essentially two distinct types of explosion: high-order and low-order. The difference is the speed of blast wave generated. Blasts that exceed the speed of sound are considered high-order. Pipe bombs, gunpowder, and Molotov cocktails produce low-order explosions. TNT, C-4, nitroglycerin, and dynamite produce high-order explosions — technically, supersonic over-pressurization shock waves. You won't hear them coming; their blast will be upon you before their bang. The damage arrives before the warning. And the damage is different: the impact of the blast itself can cause significant injury to ears, lungs, abdomen, and brain – some not evident until hours or days after the event.

Anger also comes in different speeds. Sometimes it builds like a pressure-cooker, with ample audible and visible alarms available well before the threshold of danger is breached. You may notice someone getting angry and angrier, and still feel you have time to "talk them down" before they lose their composure. And then there are the other times, when the increasing concentration of silent rage shows no outward signs. No indication is given of impending destruction. Time bombs don't always tick, and anger doesn't always give notice. The volatility is invisible. Fast anger is dangerous not only because the object has no time to prepare or react, but even more because the subject has no time to restrain or redirect. It just happens too fast.

I'm not sure which troubled me more: that I had hit him in a violent and dangerous attack, or that I had no awareness or memory of having done it. I would add, almost parenthetically, that he was okay; but I'm not actually sure that would be completely true. A lot changed that day — in me, perhaps in him, and most certainly in the relationship between us. A new variable was introduced that day, one that was rarely if ever discussed, but most certainly never forgotten.

Occasionally I hear people say about someone they know, "He (or she) is simply not the kind of person that could do such a thing." I have come to believe that is another way of saying that the rage was undetectable, and the detonator concealed. Everyone is capable, whether they can imagine it or not. I've also noticed that the book of Genesis gives a very scant and unsatisfying explanation for what led Cain to the level of anger that he could murder his brother Abel. The distinction between God's pleasure at their respective sacrifices does not in any way connect all the dots. As with much ancient scripture, more truth is contained in what is left unexplained than in the sketchy details preserved. We simply don't know what Cain was thinking or feeling. Abel didn't know either, and didn't see it coming. Cain may not have seen it coming himself, even as it came into him and through him. High-order explosions happen too fast. No one gets any warning.

James was arguably the most practical — some would say utilitarian — of the Biblical writers. He did not advise his readers to avoid getting angry; he counseled them to get there slowly. Develop better sensors, cultivate a longer fuze, identify and uncover the trip wires, and try to keep any blasts at a sub-sonic velocity. Give the folks around you a chance to take cover, and give yourself a chance to contain the damage.

There's another side to the speed of anger. Once the burn has been initiated, even a low-order explosion cannot be suppressed or contained completely. Simmering ordnance can remain unstable for a very long time — years, even decades are possible. Even specialists trained in Explosive Ordnance Disposal typically can't make volatile devices safe; instead, they blow the things up, containing the damage by all means available. They essentially create controlled crises, rather than toy with the futile effort of avoiding "sudden moves" in perpetuity. Unexploded ordnance is going to blow up, sooner or later, one way or another. Unresolved anger will do the same. Don't just let it simmer, hoping it will go away on its own, or somebody is going to get hurt. Paul, a writer of dramatically different disposition than James, encouraged his readers to get angry, but not to stay angry. Get angry, but don't sin. Don't do anything you'll regret later. Get angry, and then get rid of your anger, before the sun sets. That's strong advice —

with a lifetime of mortal confrontation, unjust imprisonment, and the passionate opposition of former allies contributing to his wisdom.

Some people try to get rid of anger by imploding, rather than exploding. They would rather absorb the damage themselves than risk harming the people around them. These are the people that will throw themselves under a bus, jump on their own hand grenades, and confess to crimes they didn't commit — all in distorted efforts to spare others from a seething rage. There is something tragically noble about this peculiar form of self-sacrifice. Greater love has not been known, than to lay down one's life for a friend... and yet the distortion is most troubling. There's a chance that nobody will be helped by your suffering, no one healed by your scars, no soul saved by your death. Too many have been led to their own private crucifixions by voices not from God, seeking a redemption that cannot be delivered by their own hands.

Depression is often characterized as anger turned inward. From what I have seen in my years among people, this phenomenon has surpassed the scale of epidemic, and can now be considered a statistical norm. The consequences are legion, and tomes have been written to catalog their range. People are angry at themselves, in every direction you look, in every aspect of your life. Treatments are available, therapies ubiquitous, and empathetic support in every extended family or circle of friends. What more can be done?

Anger has to go somewhere. Even Jesus did not extinguish the demons that possessed the tortured Gesarene; he sent them into a herd of pigs. It seems to be an odd corollary to the first law of thermodynamics, that this sort of energy is neither created nor destroyed. It has to go somewhere. Unresolved anger, like unexploded ordnance, cannot safely be ignored. The thing is going to blow, sooner or later, somehow or other. The best we can do may be to create controlled crises as needed, and minimize the damage by all means available.

Don't suppress your anger. You can't. Don't absorb your anger. It will destroy you and the people you love. Slow your anger, and stretch the time available to deal with its dangers. Express your anger, before it gets the best of you. But don't stop at expressing. Channel your anger, direct your anger, master your anger. Send it where you want it to go. Use it to destroy what needs to be destroyed, and to create what longs to be created. And move the world with your passion.

Notes about Anger

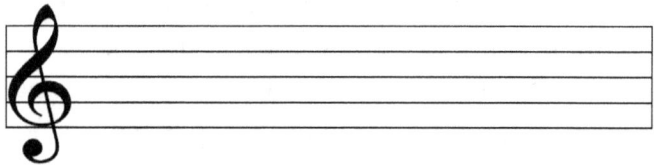

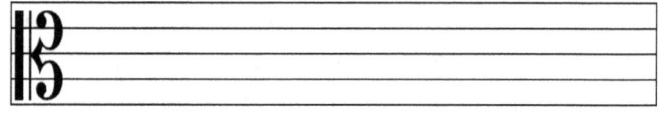

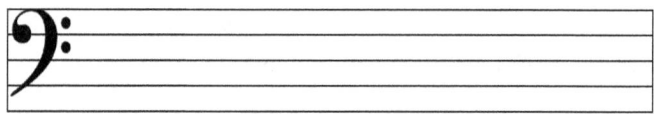

G – GRASPING PEACE

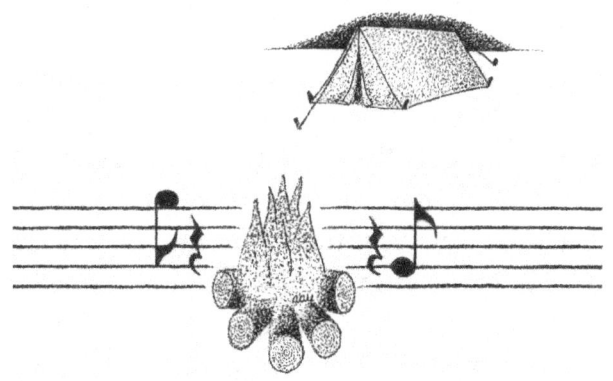

> *I have said these things to you,*
> *That in me you may have peace.*
> *In the world you will have tribulation.*
> *But take heart; I have overcome the world.*
> *(John 16:27, NASB)*

The most at rest my soul has ever been was atop a deeply familiar outcropping just south of the Appalachian Trail, near the top of the western slope of Thunderhead Mountain. I was there just before sunset, leading a small contingent of my scout troop on a four-day backpacking trip in the Great Smoky Mountains, nearing our first night's rest at the Spence Field trail shelter. Clear views from that wondrous vantage point are not taken for granted, for you never know when or whether such a sight shall be offered. It cannot be timed or predicted, it cannot be planned. And should you ever meet such good fortune, I assure you that you will not be prepared for what your eyes shall receive.

I was granted this long-awaited gift in mid-October, when colors cascade through countless ridges and autumn transforms the understanding of life itself. No artist's brush nor camera's lens can ever quite capture the impact on the soul of witnessing such vast beauty. Fontana Lake, perhaps 30 miles south, beckoned as an oasis of tranquility beyond the radiant canopies, and I could either hear or feel the footsteps of ten thousand pilgrims descending to her shores — with ten thousand more bidding her adieu to seek the lofty palace upon which I then stood. I stopped, completely stopped, in nothing less than reverence of worship. I laid down my backpack, took off my boots, and sat in awestruck wonder.

I had absolutely no desire to leave, or to be in any other place but there. Sunset approached, which promised even more transfixing beauty, even as it warned of darkness, and many unseen dangers to travelers still on the trail. My fellow adult leader sensed my deep desire to watch the sun until its last glimmer, and graciously offered to lead the troop on to the shelter, less than two miles away down a gentle slope. I would follow later, along a well-traveled trail that I had known since childhood. I knew better. It was not a wise choice to remain alone there, and to hike alone that last stretch of trail as darkness overwhelmed the fading light. Yet my soul longed to stay, so stay I did, and witnessed a sunset I shall not even attempt to describe.

Don't ask me how, but somehow, I knew that would be my last time on Rocky Top. The seconds passed slowly and silently, and the moment lingers still. Then the sun set, and darkness overflowed the valleys, ascending steep slopes with stealth and resolve. I slipped my feet back into my boots, hoisted the pack onto replenished shoulders, and moved quickly down the trail. Off to the north, with what little light remained, I started to notice an ocean of dense white mist pour over the distant ridges, filling the valley beneath me. Before I could gauge its approaching pace, it was upon me, and I could see only where my next step would land upon the rocky dirt illuminated briefly by my flashlight's narrow beam. I could also see my own foolishness. (I didn't need the flashlight for that.)

I did not sense fear, nor anxiety — not yet. I was caught up in the wonder and awe of the extremes, of how the most spectacular view ever revealed to me had so quickly and completely become concealed. I now was nearly blind, when so recently I could see more than I could perceive. I traveled on, with mind and soul in flight, hoping mostly to remember all that was present to me at that time. A few rocks here and there escaped my notice, which my ankle did not appreciate, but my body continued to do what it knew to do, as my mind wandered through unseen mists beyond.

My mind wandered too much, and I walked right past the path to Spence Field. It may have been 15 minutes or more before I realized the ground was too level, and the path too easy. I was no longer descending Thunderhead Mountain, and my troop was now behind me, certainly sheltered and anxiously awaiting my arrival. I raced back on the easy trail, the fog having lifted slightly, wondering how I could have possibly missed what had always been a well-marked turn. I don't know how far past I had gone or how long it took me to double back, but I remember distinctly the tremendous relief when at last I saw the clearly marked path to the shelter. To add to my sense of foolishness, there in the center of that intersection stood a small sapling with a forked trunk, holding a fallen branch at just the right angle, as if shouting to anyone paying attention, "Turn Here!"

I turned indeed, and raced on a hundred yards or so to the trail shelter, where the rest of my troop awaited — some sleeping, some tending the welcome fire. But the look of relief on those who saw me first was mixed, and confused, and I quickly learned why. "Where's Alex?!", they asked.

Alex, my son, had grown worried about me. He had taken his friend Chris to go look for me, back up towards Rocky Top, where they had seen me last.

My voice carries well. I learned how to project from the diaphragm, both in singing and in barking orders in the Army. Never has my voice carried further nor more forcefully than it did for the eternity of the next 20 minutes. Every bear and bobcat from Fontana to Newfound Gap knew I was there, and they knew I was looking for Alex. And God help the creature that dared to come between me and my son.

I cannot begin to describe what I felt in those moments. Perhaps I don't need to; perhaps you already know. Every note on the scale of expression converged into one singular mission. And then I heard it — the unmistakable voice of my son, calling out in response. We guided each other loudly through the darkness, until the faint beams of flashlights could be discerned.

I saw enough beautiful sights that day to fill an album of replenishing memory, but none more moving, more memorable, more transformative than the barely perceivable faces of my son and his friend. We embraced, and laughed, and talked over each other with stories and explanations, and I don't remember a single detail of it, except that we looked for each other, and found each other.

I began by saying that my soul was never more at rest than it was that evening on Rocky Top. That wasn't true. The most my soul has ever been at rest was that same night, when I found my son, and he found me. We walked back to the shelter — or maybe we floated or flew, I can't remember. The others joined in our joy and relief, and I believe we all slept very well that night.

The next morning, we were off again. I think I offered them all an apology for my foolishness, along with a humble refresher course on why you never hike alone. But I received an even more enduring reminder that night: a memory of seeing and not seeing, of loss and restoration, of seeking and finding.

The journey of peace begins when you understand most clearly what you are searching for.

Notes about Peace

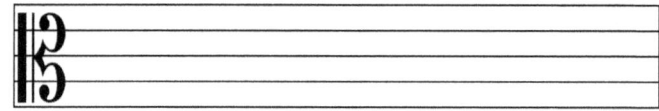

G# – THE CUP OF LONELINESS

> *About the ninth hour Jesus cried out with a loud voice,*
> *Saying, "Eli, Eli, lama sabachthani?"*
> *That is, "My God, my God, why have you forsaken me?"*
> *(Matthew 27:46, NASB)*

It was Thanksgiving, my favorite holiday of the year. But it wasn't Thanksgiving there, not where I was. I was spending a semester of my sophomore year overseas, in the beautiful old city of Dijon, France, while attending classes at the University of Dijon. I spent every weekend in a different city, sometimes arriving at the train station on Friday afternoon with an overnight bag and only the faintest notion of which destination I might choose.

I did not mind traveling alone, although I often longed to have someone to share the experience with: the full moon hovering in the midst of the clear night sky of Chamonix, with the overwhelming beauty of the French Alps shimmering in the background; the Chateaux de Chenonceau in the Loire valley, with its ethereal design of symmetrical gardens and opulent décor; the Jet d'Eau fountain in Geneva, Switzerland, an embodiment of vibrant tranquility in the quintessential home of peace itself.

I knew then in part what I know now more fully: that life at any time in any place overflows with opportunity to experience beauty, and grandeur, and transcendent inspiration. Yet with that opportunity always comes risk. The range and diversity of threats — dangers from without and from within — far exceed what any of us are prepared for.

There was a partial train strike on the Sunday that I returned from Saint Tropez, that precious gem on the French Mediterranean. It was also conscription day, that day each year when all the young men who had turned 18 were to report to a regional station to begin their mandatory service. There was only one train going north that day, and the phrase "standing room only" was further compressed by each added traveler, pushing somewhat desperately to claim a fraction of a square meter for themselves. The train moved slowly when it moved at all, and even moved backwards once for quite a while, as if in leaderless indecision about its next destination.

I was just familiar enough with southern France to recognize that the station we were entering was not on the route to Dijon, but perhaps 100 km northeast of it, with tracks leading further from where I needed to be. My own indecision caused almost too much delay, as I elbowed my way to the end of the rail car, leaping off as the train began its accelerating departure. Somehow, through the auditory chaos of that instant, I heard a loud voice calling out indiscernible words in my direction. I turned to see a young man waving my passport and my wallet, which must have fallen out of my pocket during my frantic exit. Once eye contact was made, he reached out as far as he could, then tossed them with impressive accuracy into my anxious hands. I don't know how I could ever learn the name of that foreign friend, but his strong initiative and alert kindness will not soon be forgotten.

There were other adventures, to be told on other days, but what strikes me now in the telling is how very alone I was, in a quite distant land. I was not bothered at the time by my aloneness, partly because I was naive, and in larger part because I always found myself among good people. I found so very many of the people I met to be kind and gracious, welcoming and generous, thoughtful and understanding. A young man from Algiers, whom I met at a hostel in Paris, introduced me to some of his friends who shared our love of music. Yes, I had brought my banjo with me, and he and I one evening played guitar and banjo for a large and appreciative gathering on the plaza in front of the Cathedral of Notre Dame. As the crowd of students grew in size and in festivity, a small phalanx of gendarmes gave us a quick and succinct reminder that the freedom of assembly was not guaranteed in this place, and thus the serendipitous concert came to an abrupt end.

Yes, this place was different, and as much as I loved it — and all the adventures it launched — it was not my home. It was most especially not my home on Thanksgiving Day, a few short weeks from the end of my stay. Technically, it wasn't Thanksgiving there. I cannot comprehend all that Einstein explained about the phenomenal connection between space and time, but on that day, I sensed quite profoundly that being in a different place caused it to be a different time.

It was my first Thanksgiving away from home, and being away from home that day felt an awful lot like being nowhere at all. I spent most of the day at a local park; I believe it was Jardin Darcy, near the train station, but I don't remember clearly. The park was beautiful and beautifully kept, as all of the parks and gardens in France seemed always to be. I don't believe I sensed the presence of another soul in the park that day, and my solitude grew within me the more that I reflected on it.

I had by that time become functionally fluent in French. (I had studied it for seven years before living there.) As I have heard others affirm with equal amazement, there is a point, after spending a few months living in another language, that you begin to think and dream in that language. I had hit that point, and found that I rarely needed to resort to my English repository of words to find a way to express my thoughts. That day was such a rare time, for I simply could not find any way to express in French the feelings that occupied my mind. It wasn't just solitude or homesickness that I felt; it was some other aspect of my aloneness that was eating away at my suddenly fragile happiness. After much discordant reflection, I eventually reached back into English thoughts and stumbled upon the phrase that fit: I did not feel needed. To this day, I don't know how to express that thought in French, for in that corner of the world a need is something you have, not something you feel. The closest I could come to the French version of the thought was that there was no one at that time who had any need of me.

I could and would spend my entire day at that park, and no one anywhere would be wondering where I was, what I was doing, or whether I was okay. Such a thing simply would not occur back home in Knoxville, and most certainly not on Thanksgiving Day. And just as the thought had searched for a phrase, now the phrase in turn sought and found a feeling. I was feeling lonely. Far beyond alone, distant, or isolated — I was lonely in a way I had never before felt or imagined. At that moment in that place, I did not matter to anyone. Not in a tragic or depressive sense, but in a sterile objective rationality, I reached the inevitable conclusion that I was unimportant, at least momentarily. How long that moment would last was not yet clear. In hindsight, it did not last very long, but its memory has lingered now for 40 years.

At that age, I had barely begun my readings and reflections of philosophy, and I had barely made the acquaintance of existentialist thought. But there in that park, on that lonely day, the seeds of understanding were planted, which later grew. I had not yet encountered any "dark night of the soul", nor had I considered the vast emptiness of human spirits, nor witnessed the despair of souls crushed under the apparent meaninglessness of their own existence. But as I continued to grow, and age, and connect with lives increasingly different from my own, I came to recognize this common thread in so many of our fabrics.

We desperately need to feel needed, passionately want to feel wanted, and intensely love to feel loved. The barren lack of any or all of those things is utterly depleting, and drains from our reserves the very energy from which life springs. Emptiness within our core often triggers involuntary urgency, as surely as emptiness in our lungs demands immediate gasping for air. And yet oddly, emptiness can sometimes be foolishly ignored, and loneliness irresponsibly neglected or numbed. Loneliness is itself an empty cup, a vessel only useful when empty, when not filled with things of lesser value than what we long for most.

If I may offer a self-contradictory wish for you, I wish that you might never feel lonely, or empty, or meaningless... but in the same caring breath, I also wish that you might taste the cup of loneliness, if only to know its strength, sense its fullness, and ponder its timeless and unbounded meaning.

Notes about Loneliness

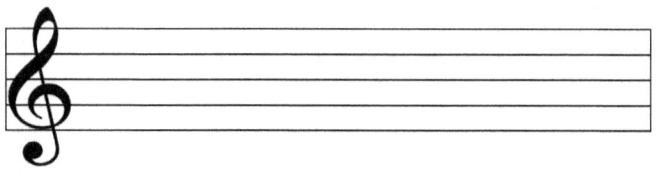

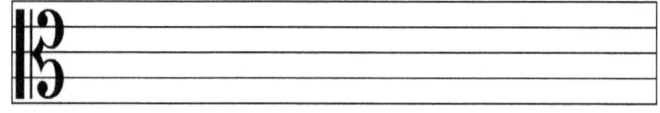

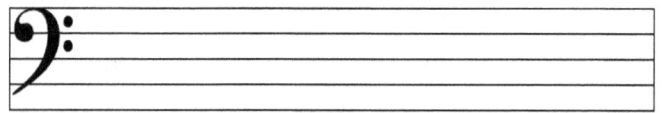

A – APPROACHING INTIMACY

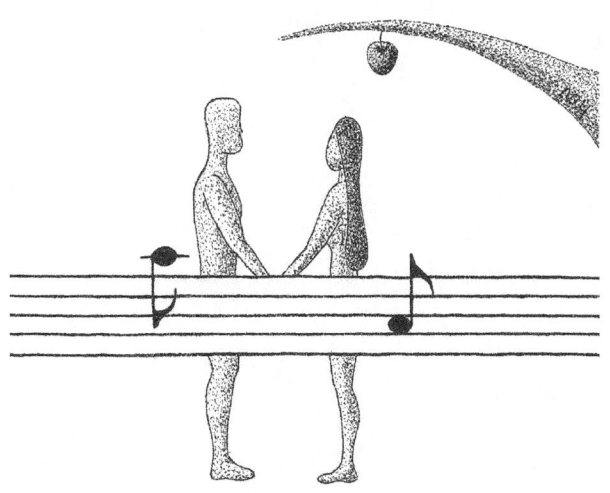

> *Then the man said,*
> *"This at last is bone of my bones,*
> *And flesh of my flesh;*
> *She shall be called Woman,*
> *Because she was taken out of Man."*
> *Therefore a man shall leave his father and his mother*
> *And hold fast to his wife,*
> *And they shall become one flesh.*
> *And the man and his wife were both naked*
> *And were not ashamed.*
> *(Genesis 2:23-25, NASB)*

"I know you, Mom."

That was my last and definitive argument against my mother's firm insistence that she would never ever treat anyone that way — the way that her caregiver for the evening, and others before her, had patiently endured and reported. My mother is scared at times, as any reasonable soul would be, facing similar circumstances. She acts out of that fear with authentic passion, as unfiltered as any thought that crosses her mind and her lips in rapid succession. She can be belligerent, combative, feisty, defiant... and painfully, refreshingly honest. Then after an hour or a day, she may not remember even being upset, and will apologize with sincere regret for any trouble she has caused.

My mother despises the loss of control over her own life and home, as I despise being a party and a witness to that loss. I never wanted to see this day come, and most certainly neither did she... yet she saw that it was coming, and I see now that it is indeed here. She prepared for this day, and courageously taught me what I should do when it came. She worked out the details of what the next step would be, and left it up to me to know when to take it. She knew that she would someday lose the ability to care for my father and for herself, and so chose a facility where the transitions — from independent to assisted, from assisted to skilled care — might be most easily made. And because she is honest, except when she's lying (she readily admits that she lies a lot), I am able to see clearly that someday has arrived.

I know her, and she knows me.

There were too many decades when I did not believe either of those things to be true. I felt as if we were strangers, neither able to connect to the other in terms of interests or fears, ambitions or concerns. My first wife also fell into that distance, that alienation. She and my mother never actually knew each other, never developed any fondness or understanding for the other, which both accentuated and contributed to the weakness of our marriage.

In ways that I never expected and most certainly cannot explain, it seemed to be the occasion of my divorce that opened up a fresh opportunity for me to know my mother, and for her to know me. Perhaps in part it was my inescapable vulnerability, my grave fear that I had been a disappointment to my parents, that provided my mother a window through which to show me her unconditioned support and unqualified love. Many among my friends and acquaintances treated the divorce as a contagion, an unwelcome revelation, and sufficient cause to lose interest in me and my life thereafter. My mother went the opposite direction, revealing much more of her own story than she ever had before, and truly nurturing my every hopeful thought, encouraging my every hesitant step to rebuild my patterns, my passions, and my life. She urged patience and caution on any new relationships, and let me know when she thought I was ready to risk loving again. She knew me a lot better than I realized. Any by some wondrous mystery, I began to realize that I knew her far better than I had suspected... a truth that was slowly revealed in parallel with my openness with her.

My mother tells me toward the end of almost every conversation we have that she is glad that I am her son, and I tell her that I am glad she is my mother. Even in the conversation we had to have today —- the one where I told her it was time, the time that she had dreaded yet prepared for years ago — she said it again, and I said it too. And it was even more true today than yesterday.

I know that this move will be good for her, in ways that are impossible to be happy about. Dad will move to a skilled care room, where there are people well trained and attentive to the needs of dementia patients. Mom will move to an assisted living apartment (room, more accurately) where she will be just down the hall from Dad, able to visit him any time, eat meals with him, sit together, and be together. And she won't have the house to worry about any more, or laundry, or dishes, or dust, or any of those things... or a home. Am I saying that too strongly? She is going to lose her home, the place she knows as home. In a fit of frustration a few weeks ago, she told me she was tired of the rules and the nurses and the worries, and that she and Dad were going to leave and move back home to Knoxville — to the home I grew up in, from birth through high school, a house which they hadn't seen in roughly 40 years.

Home carries a lot of meaning, and a lot of different meanings. More than any other association, I believe that Home is the place that you know most well, and where you are most well known. Perhaps Mom is not going to lose her home in that sense, but simply move it — into a much smaller space. Honestly, I can't process that right now... not yet.

There is a piece of this story that I need to share now, perhaps a few paragraphs out of place. That time I mentioned earlier, when my mother assured me enough time had passed, and that I could risk loving again... she knew at that time, and had known for some time, that I had indeed fallen in love. When the time was right, my mother was very anxious to meet this wonderful lady. So anxious, in fact, that she and Dad flew from California to Kentucky to meet her. To say that my mother bonded with her quickly would be an extraordinary understatement. I don't know that five minutes had passed before they were exchanging knowing looks and verbal shorthand that let me know they already knew things about each other that I had not yet even suspected. They made a connection in their first encounter that has done nothing but grow and strengthen in the years since.

My wife knows and understands my mother in ways that amaze and instruct me. She helps me see things from her perspective, imagine her fondest hopes, and pay attention to her deepest concerns. Truth be known, it is because of my wife that I truly learned to know my mother, and because of my mother that I have been better able to know my wife.

Knowing is the heart of intimacy. Understanding the limits of our understanding, and embracing the authentic desire to know fully — and be known fully — this is the purest and deepest craving of our souls. Reaching far beyond the scope of romantic bonds, intimacy speaks to our capacity to know and be known without masks, without pretense, without even the strength to conceal our deficiencies and vulnerabilities. Intimacy bears the weighty burden of risk: that being known might destroy the possibility of being loved, and that knowing fully might make loving fully impossible to achieve.

And yes, within those romantic boundaries, intimacy speaks to knowing and loving without fig leaves, without self-consciousness or concealment, without deception or distrust. If the ultimate expression of the love of God is found in God's unfathomable self-revelation, then so also is our deepest act of love and self-expression to be found in our unconstrained revelation of who we are, as we are, to those by whom we most especially want to be fully known.

Intimacy also entails being unconstrained and unfiltered in our passions and desires. To pull it off, we have to find that mysterious confidence and trust that our desires will converge — and not conflict — with the unfettered desires of the ones we love. When that convergence actually occurs, and the risk is in fact rewarded, I don't know what to call it, other than miraculous.

Intimacy may well be the most private of all our experience, and yet it affects everything we do and every relationship we have. Because my wife knows me well, and knows my mother, she was able to share words and thoughts that might help ease my mother's mind, and help her understand the need for this next move. And of course, she was right.

The thoughts and words of my dear wife were at the same time authentically hers and authentically mine, because they sprang from a common love, a shared understanding, and a deeply intertwined way of experiencing the difficulties that lie ahead. My wife knew what my mother's reaction would be because she knows her heart, shares her concern, and wishes for her happiness with a sincerity that rings true in my mother's ear.

There is a reverberation to intimacy, a harmonic resonance to deep knowing. We often refer to this as being in tune with each other, on the same wavelength, communicating on the same frequency. When I tune a banjo, I know I have tuned it well if the high-D first string vibrates when the low-D fourth string is plucked. We have a remarkable capacity to tune ourselves to each other, in ways that genuinely cause us to sense each vibration in the soul of those we love.

My wife and I will be driving to North Carolina this week, to help my Mom and Dad transition into their new homes. I have no idea what words will be spoken, or how many tears shed, but I have trust and confidence that the thoughts shared will be understood, and that the impulses felt will be somehow quietly shared.

Notes about Intimacy

A# – THE KNOTS OF ANXIETY

> *Be anxious for nothing,*
> *But in everything by prayer and supplication with thanksgiving*
> *Let you requests be made known to God.*
> *And the peace of God, which surpasses all comprehension,*
> *Will guard your hearts and minds in Christ Jesus.*
> *(Philippians 4:6-7, NASB)*

My stomach was in knots, as was my mind.

Knot ready.
Knot willing.
Knot able.
Knot effective.

No, I didn't misspell those knots. There is simply a difference between lacking whatever it is you need and having it, yet finding it to be so twisted, tangled, and tight as to be essentially unusable. Anxiety is not composed of emptiness, ignorance, and apathy. Quite the contrary, anxiety is the perception of having almost everything that is needed at the time, but not quite enough of it. It is essentially frustrated enthusiasm, full of tenacious attempts to engage mind, will, and body in some seemingly urgent endeavor, but without the traction necessary to plow through the mud and ice.

My most disastrous experience with anxiety was fortunately a fictitious one, an all-too-realistic training exercise with dummy ammunition, and very little actual risk of harm. I was cast in the role of platoon leader, on a routine troop movement through a moderately wooded area. The sound that suddenly echoed off of each and every tree was that of sniper fire, repeating at unpredictable intervals from indiscernible directions. I cannot begin to describe the impact those sounds had on my immediate capacity to think or move. For all practical purposes, I was immobile and unconscious, or so it surely seemed to those temporarily placed under my trial command. Among those was a seasoned combat veteran from two tours in Viet Nam. He assessed the situation quickly, made eye contact with me that let me clearly and confidently know that he was assuming command. He led the unit skillfully out of the woods and to the end of the training exercise. My evaluator made himself heard and understood by everyone in a two-mile radius, but he was only talking to me. I had just killed every soldier in my unit.

I was not ready for that — for the exercise, for the deservedly brutal critique, or for the truth about myself that lodged itself permanently in the depths of my psyche. I was unprepared, in every sense of the word. It was not that I lacked training, but that whatever training I had been given became oddly inaccessible at the very moment I needed it. I was insecure, self-conscious, and full of self-doubt when the situation called for me to be strong, steady, and confident.

I was not willing to do what needed to be done, when it needed to be done most urgently. I wasn't willing to take the risk that absolutely needed to be taken: the risk of being wrong, of choosing a wrong direction, of leading my unit into even greater peril. I was indecisive, paralyzed by my own uncertainty, and grossly lacking the force of will to lead with determination and resolve.

I was not able to tell where the shots were coming from, where the sniper might be, which route through the woods would prove least fatal. I could not solve the puzzle, could not figure out the answer. I was inadequate, coming up short in every category, and rightfully humiliated in front of my peers and rivals. It was probably then that the U.S. Army decided with great wisdom that I was not cut out to command a combat unit; I clearly did not have the right stuff. (They ended up assigning me to an analysis team, in a school setting, where I wrote statistical simulations and management software for ammunition logistics — a much better fit for my limited abilities.)

I was not effective in a combat leadership role. I was incompetent, and worse than useless. My mission resulted in catastrophic failure. People died, in a sense that only combat simulations and well-staged training exercises can produce. I cannot even guess the number of times that I have thanked God that my failure came in training rather than in combat, and that I was never put into any situation where my indecision could result in the actual loss of life or limb.

The experience of that hour has remained with me vividly for nearly 40 years now. The fact that it was fictitious — a simple simulation with no real danger — has also shed light on the nature of anxiety itself. Anxiety works almost exclusively within the realm of perception, without regard to its connection with reality. If we perceive danger, we respond with equal alertness and heightened awareness, whether that danger turns out to be real or imagined. So also with perceptions of ourselves: if we for any reason find ourselves feeling insecure, indecisive, inadequate, or ineffective, then at that point it matters not how others perceive us, or how we might fare on some hypothetically objective measure of our performance or worth. In terms of the debilitating impact of anxiety, it matters only how we perceive ourselves, and the situation we believe ourselves to be in. This is precisely what ties the knot, springs the trap, and gets us mired in the inescapably muddy maze. It simply does not help to consider anxiety as an irrational response, for it is very clearly the only rational response, if the situation even might be what we perceive and believe it to be.

Another highly anxious event came our way last week, as my wife and I moved my parents into a nursing home. All the same questions appeared, but this time it was not a simulation. Was I ready? I was not at all prepared for the many unexpected events and echoes of distant painful memories. I was overwhelmed and exhausted, from many angles, at many times. Was I willing? In no way was this something I wanted to do, and at no point did the decisions seems sufficiently clear. Was I able? My parents are both extraordinarily strong-willed individuals, and at no time did I feel capable of persuading or forcing either of them to do anything they did not want to do.

Was I effective? I do not know how to answer the final question. By the time we left, both Mom and Dad were settled in their new environments. Dad was no longer pushing me away or standing stubbornly immovable. Mom was no longer demanding to speak to her lawyer or cursing at the nurses. In fact, as we said goodbye for now, it struck me deeply that both Mom and Dad seemed happier, more relaxed, more outgoing, and more at peace that I have seen them in years, if not decades. I simply don't know exactly how that happened.

Perhaps I was ready enough, willing enough, and able enough. Perhaps enough truly is enough, and sufficiency is the only question that really matters. Sufficient to each day is the evil it bears, and sufficient is God's grace to our every need. Anxiety doesn't go away, not even on a good day. It lingers and loiters, sometimes hiding in dark corners of self-doubt and self-consciousness. One learns to cope with it, to battle it from day to day, understanding that simply overcoming it for that day, for that battle, for that moment, can be enough for now.

From the midst of my own forty-year battle with anxiety in many forms, I feel an impulse to share here a handful of suggestions that have helped me along the way, in hopes that they may be somewhat helpful to you as well:

1) Surround yourself with beauty. I'm not exactly sure why, but beauty in many modes - sunsets and mountain streams, sandy beaches and symphonies, paintings and classic sculpture - seem to remind me that there is very much good in the world, which serves to counter my tendency to despair.

2) Play, just for fun. I typically don't keep score in golf or in tennis, just to reinforce the idea that I'm doing both for fun, not for accomplishment. Less goal-oriented activity and more spontaneous adventure get me out of the mode of trying too hard, and keep the fear of failure out of the equation.

3) Push back on expectations. I don't mind the pressure of the commitments I've made, to people I've chosen to serve. It's the expectations that come on their own, from people I never offered to help or expected to please, that seem endlessly draining. Resign from jobs you never accepted, withdraw from causes you never joined, and freely disappoint people you never agreed to satisfy.

4) Honor your own needs. It's clearly not wrong to be hungry or thirsty. Nor is it wrong to need rest, or encouragement, or medication, or counseling. You have better insights into your own needs than anyone else does. Pay attention to them.

5) Choose your companions. Some people replenish you, some drain you, and some walk beside you faithfully in every circumstance. You know who they are. Spend time with the people who bring out the best in you.

6) Free your thoughts, even the dark ones. Ignore the voices that tell you everything is going to be okay; not everything will be. Bad stuff will happen, along with the good. Allow your mind to face the truth of what's possible, not without fear, but in spite of it. You have faced tough stuff before. You will again.

7) Breathe in both directions: inhale and exhale. Take in what you need, release what you don't. Receive

and give help, in equal measure. Don't hold your breath. Let it flow in and out. Find a rhythm that works for you, and trust it.

Notes about Anxiety

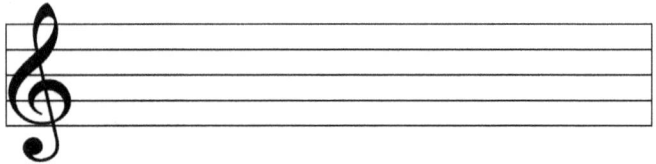

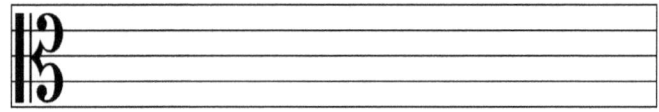

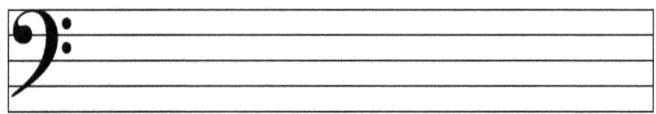

B – BUILDING UPON GRATITUDE

> *Enter His gates with thanksgiving*
> *And His courts with praise.*
> *Give thanks to Him, bless His name.*
> *For the* L*ORD* *is good;*
> *His lovingkindness is everlasting*
> *And His faithfulness to all generations.*
> *(Psalm 100:4-5, NASB)*

As I ponder the times and situations when gratitude resonated most deeply within me, the occasions are quite numerous, and the circumstances widely varied.

I think of the time our minivan broke down two hours from our Louisville home, at two o'clock in the morning. We were already exhausted from a week of camping and the long drive home from Colorado. Before cell phones populated the earth or cars communicated with satellites, this meant a nervous venture down the road in search of a pay phone.

I was thankful that I found one about two miles away, even more grateful that a local towing company answered the call and came promptly. There were no repair shops open at that hour, but the tow truck driver knew the manager of a decent hotel in the next town, right next to a repair shop that would open in the morning. Somehow, he fit my wife, my three sons and I into the cab of his truck, hauled us with our broken vehicle into town, and persuaded the manager to put us up for the night at half the normal cost. I wasn't sure how to thank him, for our cash was quite depleted by our Rocky Mountain vacation, and our credit as exhausted as we were.

I was thankful beyond words when my friend Chuck was able to borrow the church van the next morning to come retrieve us and all our gear. I thanked the hotel manager for his generosity, and the manager of the auto repair shop for allowing us to leave our minivan in his parking lot until we could find a way to pay for the repairs. And I thanked Chuck for coming to our rescue, and for taking us home.

I was somewhat awestruck and deeply appreciative when, upon our arrival home, we found in our mailbox an unexpected offer for a quick and easy home refinance, designed to take advantage of falling interest rates. I was beyond thankful that it was in fact both quick and easy, and that the math worked out to also pull enough equity out of our home to repair and retrieve our damaged vehicle.

I was speechless when I learned that there would also be just enough money left over to take the first step towards starting my own business, a dream that had been growing within me for over four years, and which had become more pressing when I learned that my current job was in jeopardy. That urgency grew when I listened to a recorded phone message, which informed me that the church in Wyoming that had just interviewed me — and the only church that had expressed any interest in me at all in the four months since my graduation from seminary — decided that I was not the man they wanted as their pastor. (Apparently my views on divorced people serving as deacons were too moderate for the majority of their members.)

I started my business because my car broke down in the middle of the night, and because I was too broke to get it fixed, and because a church in Wyoming didn't choose me as their pastor. These ended up being some of the best things that ever happened to me, and I shall always be deeply grateful to the many folks who went far out of their way to help us, every step of the way.

There are many other stories to tell that fit a similar pattern. Stories of reaching the end of my own resourcefulness, nervous and lost about what to do next, only to find somewhere in each maze of anxiety a particular set of people seemingly prepared for just such a need, very able and very willing to help me in ways far beyond what I deserved, far beyond my ability to repay.

Deep in the recesses of childhood memory resides another such story, one that truly marks the beginning of the most important journey of my life. It happened at the end of the Billy Graham crusade in Knoxville, in the summer of 1970. I was ten years old, and my perspective on the significance of that event in Knoxville's history was understandably naive and narrow.

Mom had taken me to the crusade on its first evening, and something stirred within my heart unlike any impulse I had ever felt before. In later years, I stumbled upon words that come close to an apt description of the feeling: it was as if an eye-hook, fastened securely to my sternum, was being pulled firmly by some thick rope, or more accurately, by some unseen hand at the other end of that rope. I wanted desperately to respond. Yet as surely as my pleading eyes conveyed to my mother my sincere desire, her firm gaze and clear brevity conveyed to me that this was not the time, and that more thought and reflection were needed for a decision such as this.

I thought of little else for days, although much was happening around me. My father, in his role at the Air National Guard base, got caught up in the controlled chaos of the U.S. Secret Service, for President Nixon had decided to attend the crusade, and Air Force One would be landing on one of my father's runways. Well, I thought of them as his runways, for he trained the tanker pilots that flew in and out of them for about 30 years. From the few morsels of information he was able to share, I gathered that it was perhaps the most stressful week of his career.

At the same time, my uncle Ed, then serving as President of the University of Tennessee, was dealing with the mounting tensions of escalating anti-war protests all over campus. The announced appearance of President Nixon at Neyland Stadium (the site of the Crusade) poured jet fuel on those angry fires of protest, and the risk of significant violence was likely greater than I can imagine.

Somehow, in the midst of all this, Mom eventually yielded to my relentless pleas that I be allowed to return to the crusade. (The tug of the rope had not in any way subsided.) She left me in the care of my older brother, Butch, who was 12, with strict instructions on where to meet her immediately after the crusade. These were different times, and neither my brother nor I thought it unusual that we should be trusted on our own, and fully expected to find our way to the designated pick-up spot at the appropriate time. We knew the area quite well, having attended many football and basketball games in that part of the campus. We frequently played tennis and basketball on courts in the vicinity, and swam often at the aquatic center just up the road. There was no apparent reason to be concerned. We knew this neighborhood as well as our own. For all practical purposes, it was our neighborhood.

But today was different. Record crowds poured into and around the stadium. A normal football crowd was 100,000 people; there were many more than that today. Tensions were high, security was tight, and I was anxious. No, not in the fearful, nervous way — I was excited. I wanted to find out who or what was pulling on that rope. The service was interminably long. If fuzzy memories are trustworthy, Jonny Cash was there. President Nixon flew in by helicopter, and spoke briefly, with people yelling things I couldn't understand. Some folks were escorted away by what looked like a lot of policemen. Ethel Waters sang "His

Eye Is On The Sparrow", George Beverley Shea sang "How Great Thou Art", and Cliff Barrows led an enormous choir in quite a number of old favorite hymns.

At long last, the sermon was over, and the time for the invitation was next. Before Dr. Graham had finished saying "Amen", I bolted from our seats high in the upper deck, down familiar ramps to the orange and white checkerboard at one end of the field. It never even occurred to me that my brother was struggling to keep up; I had never come close to outrunning him before, and I never have since. But that day I was in a hurry, and we got separated.

Counselors were positioned to speak with the throngs of people making their way to the front. I got into a line, and heard the counselor ask several people in front of me why they had come forward. I hadn't realized that I would be expected to put into words what was going on inside me. I didn't have any words for it. I thought quickly and intently. When the question was then put to me, the best words I could come up with were, "I want to quit being mean to my brother." To this day, Butch reminds me often what a profound change he noticed in me after that. He credits the change in my behavior with a change in his own thinking and direction. That affirmation has always been appreciated and meaningful to me. I know what changed that day. My heart changed.

But the crisis of that particular day was just beginning. Separated from my older brother, I was now on my own to find the place we were supposed to meet my mother — the Burger King on "The Strip", the main road on the north edge of the campus. It should have been a familiar walk, but the people and the traffic were overwhelming. I wasn't tall enough to see over anybody, and familiar landmarks seemed invisible. I couldn't see where I was going, and within a few blocks, I didn't know where I was.

I knew enough to ask a policeman for help. He kindly took the time to give me what seemed like straightforward directions, and I did my best to follow them. But not five minutes later, I was lost again, in a part of campus that was not familiar at all.

I suspect that I had wandered into the married housing area. A kind female student, noticing my bewildered look, asked me if I was lost. Cautious about speaking to strangers, I chose to be honest, and told her I was trying to get to the Burger King. She assured me warmly that it was only a few blocks away. She said that she and her husband would be very happy to give me a ride. I knew that I was not allowed to ride with strangers, and timidly asked if she could simply tell me how to walk there. Not long removed from my previous failure to follow directions, my confidence was wavering. When her husband chimed in with gentle assurances, my disciplined resistance crumbled, and I climbed nervously, yet gratefully, into their car.

The warm relief that my mother felt when she saw me must have melted any desire to fuss at me for being late, for losing sight of my brother, or for getting lost. The look of gratitude on Mom's face when she met the young couple who drove me there was the sweetest and most sincere I have ever seen. I think my mother would have adopted them both on the spot, if they would have been willing.

I too was grateful. But by that time, I had completely lost track of how many people to be grateful to. I had been lost in a neighborhood I thought I knew, in a crowd of tensions I had never seen. I was treated with more kindness and grace than I could have possibly deserved, when I was rather desperately in need of both.

My heart indeed changed that day, in more ways than one. I know that there are very many dangers and threats in this world, and many reasons to be cautious or even cynical. Yet from childhood I have been shown mercy, in many different ways by many different people. I don't have enough words to express my gratitude to all the wonderful people who have helped me along the way, who have built for me a foundation of trust and a confidence in grace.

Actually, there are only two words I can think of that come anywhere close: Thank you!

Notes about Gratitude

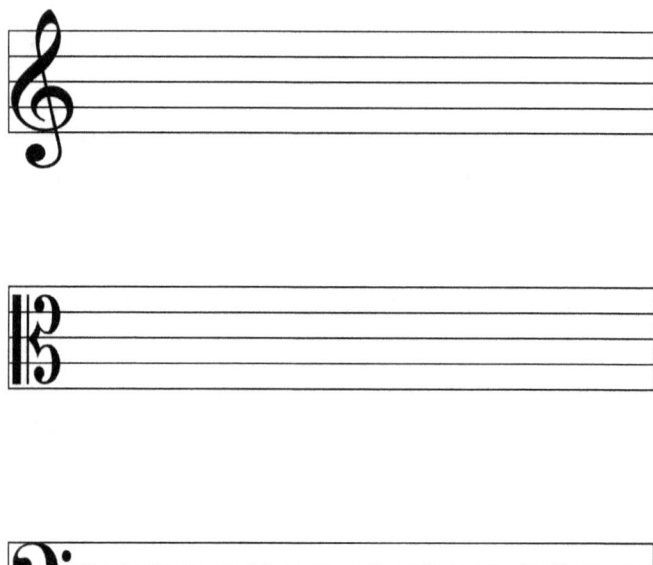

C – COMPOSING LOVE

But now faith, hope, love abide, these three;
But the greatest of these is love.
(1 Corinthians 13:13, NASB)

Anna Grace turned 13 last week, and will start middle school tomorrow. She is our next-door neighbor, along with her parents, Karen and Sam. They moved in a couple of years ago. The first time I met Anna was when she wandered into our back yard, innocently intrigued by the basketball goal on our patio. I watched eagerly as she bravely attempted a few shots, lacking the "umph" to lift it all the way to the goal. I approached gently, introduced myself, and casually lowered the goal to a more reasonable height. She shot a few more times, with only slightly more success, yet no perceptible change in her quiet determination. She caught sight of her mother walking our way, and heeded her soft encouragement to come back into their yard. Karen introduced herself timidly, apologizing for her daughter's intrusion. I assured her that no apology was necessary. I quite enjoyed sharing that brief challenge with Anna; it brought back very pleasant memories of my own childhood attempts to hoist a basketball through that intimidating hoop for the very first time. I remembered how patient my neighbor and babysitter,

Pam, had been in teaching me better techniques. It was nice to see myself on the other side of that experience, and also to see a bit of my own quiet determination in Anna's innocent and hopeful eyes.

Karen did not need to explain that Anna has the condition known as Down syndrome, which apparently has something to do with an extra copy of chromosome 21. I have not had much experience with people who have this condition, but just enough to recognize some of the patterns of expression, and also a characteristic authenticity and simplicity of manner. I would not pretend to understand the challenges or limitations faced by those with this condition, nor by those who love and care for them. Surely it must pose difficulties unlike any I have faced. The only distinction that I noticed that day was how sweet and straightforward she was, and how she, like me, struggled somewhat getting the basketball to go through the hoop.

I first met Sam a week or so later, when I noticed him in his back yard, tinkering with an outdoor swing and playset for Anna. I had heard through a friend of theirs that Sam has a few physical challenges of his own, so I was particularly curious to see if there was any way I could help. He was appreciative of the offer, but reluctant to request anything of me. We chatted briefly about our shared frustrations in assembling such contraptions, and about the nearly universal phenomenon of lacking the precise tools and hardware required by such endeavors. I went so far as to check my own modest workshop to see if I had any bolts and hex nuts that might suit the need, but I too lacked what was needed.

I don't remember if it was in that conversation or the next one that Sam shared with me a piece of his story. He had been in medical school — maybe it was his residency — when he received a diagnosis of Multiple Sclerosis. Sam had a remarkably understated way of explaining how his plans were changed by that realization. The aspect he seemed most focused on was how much more time he has now to spend with his family, and especially with Anna. Like me, Sam prefers to do as much as he can on his own, and has never asked me for help with anything. He is always gracious when I offer, but even when I watch him wrestle with his garbage can, or fumble with moving something from the car to the garage, I recognize most clearly that same quiet determination to get each task accomplished, one way or another.

My wife has gotten to know Karen better than I have, and is effusive in her praise and respect for the dear woman. Karen teaches special education in the county school system, and somehow manages always to be smiling, whether at the beginning or the end of her clearly challenging days. Karen has called us the best neighbors ever, but I think I'm getting far more of that credit than I deserve. The woman that brings me joy has also found great joy in picking out small gifts for Anna — whether for Christmas, Halloween, Easter, or just because it was cute and seemed like something Anna would like — but always finds a reason that it should be me who delivers the gift. As diligently as I might explain that my wife was the one who picked it out and wanted Anna to have it, the association has been formed that I am the bringer of gifts. I strongly suspect that is exactly the result my wife intended.

I have heard it wisely said that there is no limit to what can be accomplished if you don't care who gets the credit. I have learned by watching my wife that even greater opportunities are opened when you go out of your way to ensure the credit goes to someone else.

Last week was Anna's thirteenth birthday, and my sweet wife had prepared a gift bag of cute presents and cool back-to-school supplies. Of course, the pleasure of delivery fell to me. Sometimes Karen posts pictures and video clips of Anna opening her gifts. Her genuine excitement and simple joy is heart-warming, to say the least. A few days ago, Anna walked to our front door and rang the doorbell. I opened the door, saw her distinctive, focused, unpretentious face, and thoroughly enjoyed a brief, unhindered conversation with our precious teenage neighbor.

"I came over to say thank you for my gifts."

"That's very sweet! Did you like them?"

"Yeah," with head nodding for emphasis.

"Cool. Are you excited about going to middle school?"

"Yeah," with equal emphasis, and focused simplicity in her smile.

"Well, good! I'm glad you liked the gifts, and I'm really glad you came by!"

"Okay. Bye." And she turned to walk the twenty steps back home, but turned again before the third step to say, "I love you."

Tears almost flooded my eyes before I could gather myself to say, "I love you too."

Symphonies have been composed, masterpieces created, great works of fiction and philosophy penned from the inspiration of this universal and timeless phenomenon we know only as love. I don't know that anyone has ever expressed it as clearly, as simply, as authentically as Anna Grace.

More Notes about Love

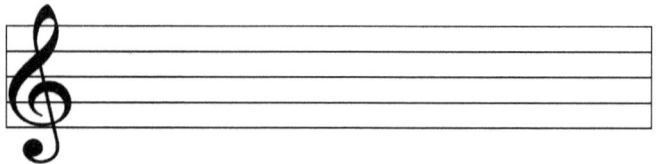

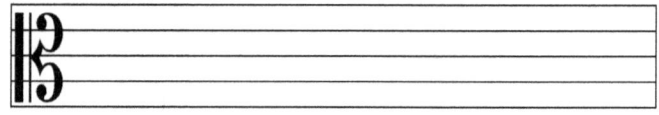

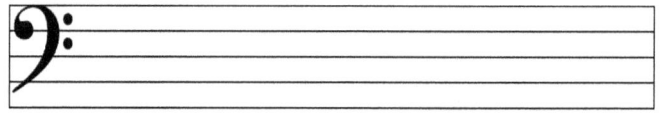

SECTION III: YOUR PART

Music seeks contact. As surely as soundwaves that never meet an ear cannot be understood as music, so expressions of thought or feeling that have no audience are essentially incomplete and unfulfilled. We wish to be heard, and to be understood. Yet we seek much more than simple contact; we seek context. We long to know how our sound resonates with the sound around us, whether in unison or parts, in harmony or discord, in conflict or communion. From the time we first become aware of our surroundings, we seek our place on the planet, our role in the play, our part in the orchestra.

Throughout junior high and high school, I was part of the youth choir at church. I use the term loosely, for my private understanding of my part in that choir was that I should be present, move my lips as if singing, and make as little sound as possible. I didn't know how to sing. Really. The few times I tried, preferably with no one in hearing range but myself, it wasn't pretty. My voice cracked often from seventh to ninth grade, I had no control of pitch or tone, and had no idea how to sustain a single note. An episode of *Gomer Pyle, USMC* caught my attention. It was the episode where Gomer (played by Jim Nabors) learned how to sing from his diaphragm. His rendition of *To Dream the Impossible Dream* still stirs my soul. I wanted to learn to sing like that, or at least to sing, from my diaphragm.

It wasn't until my senior year that I built up the nerve to ask our music minister and choir director, Dr. Carl Perry, to teach me to sing. Dr. Perry was among the most kind and understanding people I have ever known, and he picked up quickly on my trepidation and embarrassment at not knowing how to sing. He invited me to come to the church on a Sunday afternoon before choir practice started. He met me in the sanctuary, with no other ears in sight, and asked me to walk to the entrance of the center aisle... and shout. That didn't sound right, if you'll pardon the expression. I was taught to never yell in church, or even to speak above a whisper. Dr. Perry had earned my trust, so I shouted on cue. And he had me shout again, and again, sustaining the sound a little longer each time. Before long, it started to sound a little bit like a musical note. Throughout that year, he met with me just about every week, for just 15 minutes or so, and cultivated a confidence within me that I actually had a voice, that it didn't necessarily sound awful, and that there was some faint hope that I might someday be able to sing. (His confidence sounded much stronger than that; mine lagged considerably behind.)

By the time I started college, I was ready to take a big chance. I signed up for the Wake Forest Choral Union, an elective in the music department worth one hour's credit, which required passing an audition to be accepted. The day of that audition brought abundant nervousness, yet somehow a gracious conductor, John

Mochnick, saw past my awkwardness, and found room for me in the choir. I was ecstatic, stunned, and full of a new kind of nervousness: I had no idea what to expect, how my voice might blend in (or not) with the other gifted singers, how challenging or impossible my part might be.

I was surprised most of all by how the rehearsals were structured. After the initial meeting for the semester, we spent the next ten weeks or so meeting only with our sections, learning our part of Haydn's *Te Deum*. I was cast among the first basses, and found myself surrounded by rich, smooth, trained voices. Happily, I discovered that those voices belonged to people who were quite kind, patient, generous, and supportive. Little by little, I learned my part, or at least most of it. As the semester wore on, I was increasingly anxious to know what we would sound like (I liked being a part of that "we") when combined with the other sections, and then with the orchestra. That didn't happen until the dress rehearsal, just before the Christmas concert. It was, in a word, amazing. Each part blended and belonged to a masterful whole, with a power and beauty that exceeded anything I had imagined. How it happened is quite beyond my comprehension; that it happened is deeply imbedded in my memory, and in my understanding of what it means to be a part of something good. By any reasonable measure, my contribution to the whole was very small. Yet I was a part of it, and that is exactly what I wanted most to be.

HARMONY: THE ART OF BLENDING

Two weeks ago, I had the tremendous honor of standing beside a strong young marine, as we watched and patiently awaited the arrival... first of groomsmen and bridesmaids, then of best man with maid of honor, escorted also by the much cherished dog of honor, and then, at last... of his beautiful beloved bride, my treasured stepdaughter. She was stunning in every respect, an earthly embodiment of heavenly joy, grace, and boundless love. As she came into view, so also did a small pure drop of saltwater on the strong jawline of that faithful marine. The bride and her father drew slowly closer, as music played, heads turned, leaves rustled, and hearts raced. They stopped a few short paces from us, at the foot of the steps to the spacious front porch, as the familiar words flowed through my lips, "Dearly beloved, we are gathered here this day, in the sight of God and in the presence of these witnesses, to join together in holy matrimony..." The paragraph ended with the traditional question, "Who presents this woman to be married?" The beaming father answered with deep pride, humble grace, and an endearing catch in his voice, "Her mother and I."

I then invited the groom to step out and greet his bride, as I stepped aside. From there the father of the bride, also an ordained minister, continued the ceremony, as I took my seat beside the mother of the bride, my beloved wife. The one who lawfully pronounced the love-struck couple husband and wife was also my wife's ex-husband, a man whose past connected with my present in ways that were often far from pleasant. We found a way to work together — to share the stage, the roles, and the moment — to affirm and to bless the marriage of a young woman whom we each adore, to the man she now loves most of all.

It would be both dishonest and unnecessary to claim there was no tension in the event, or no difficulty to the dynamic. Of course there was. My wife inhabited the vortex of those crossed currents, and somehow managed to keep not only her balance but also her joy throughout. To the uninformed observer, I strongly suspect that everything appeared seamless and effortless. In the surrounding joy of the immediate moment, it actually felt that way. But as you surely already know, it takes hard work to make things seem easy, and considerable effort to make rough edges feel smooth. I am thankful that we were afforded the opportunity to do that work, to expend that effort, and to celebrate this wonderful event with a unity of purpose, and a common love.

Seven days ago, my brother and I did something that (somewhat strangely) neither of us had anticipated doing together. We jointly officiated the funeral of our father. The scene that seared itself into our family history, even as the first steps were taken, saw my brother and me on either side of our mother, walking her down the center aisle of a quiet chapel. She approached the casket slowly, with unwavering clarity of purpose: to tell the man she married 62 years ago that he was a good husband, that she loved him, and that she knew he loved her. With characteristic unfilteredness, she worried aloud that he was looking thin, and had lost too much weight. Then she pondered aloud that he would probably eat well now, if that is what we do up there. We spent a few minutes — I don't know how many — there together, feeling many of the same things in perhaps slightly different ways, feeling many things unique to our own relationship with the man who lay now before us.

When she was ready, and we were ready, we walked with her to our seats. A pianist played beautifully, hymns that I knew my mother loved. I played two songs on that beautiful guitar that Dad bought 50 years ago in Madrid. I read the passage in John's gospel that speaks of trusting God, of rooms being prepared, and of knowing the way. I shared vivid memories of finding the North Star by placing my head on Dad's shoulder, and following the trajectory of his arm to the light at the tip of his finger. And I pondered aloud how long and how far away the light from my father's eyes might yet be seen.

My brother shared memories of tennis and cars, of competition and tension, of learning and growing. He shared his understanding of grace, of gifts, and of life everlasting. Then he prayed, and we stood, and we walked again, he on my mother's right and I on her left, back up that same center aisle.

Outside the chapel, we stood together. We exchanged hugs and handshakes and words of grace with friends, neighbors, caregivers, and a handful of welcome strangers. We did this together, almost completely unplanned, most certainly unscripted, and in very large part unaware of what the other might say, or feel or do.

It seems awkwardly inappropriate at this point to mention that my brother and I do not have a history of working well together. In truth, it is difficult to think of anything we have done together at all. We have lived over half of our lives on different continents, and many years on different sides of this one. Even when we lived in the same house, we went to different schools, different churches, different barbers. We had different interests, different friends, different dreams. When our worlds did intersect, we often fought — physically as children, verbally as adults, and more recently with strained silence.

There is no need to explore the reasons here, nor to unpack the complex dynamics. It is enough to say that it was not clear that we would be able to overcome the tension, to care for our mother, and to care for each other, even when the need to do so was painfully clear. We were able, and I am grateful. But it would be dishonest to say the tension wasn't there, or that it didn't play a significant role in the vast range and depth of swirling emotions throughout the event.

As I was checking the tuning on my guitar, the thought occurred to me that tension is essential to any stringed instrument. A string simply dangling in air, suspended only by one end, will make no sound when struck — or if some small sound is made, it would not be mistaken for music. The tension is intentional, if you'll pardon the diction, and it needs not only to be present, but precisely the right tension, to be able to sound the notes you intend to play.

It also occurred to me that in most stringed instruments, no two strings are tuned the same. Through a combination of different composition, different lengths, and different degrees of stress, they are set up to sound different, on purpose, in order to be useful in different ways. Yet even the differences need to be precise, and precisely understood, for the strings to be useful together, in the same key or the same chords.

My brother and I are very different, and those essential differences are noticed most especially by us, and by those most dear to us. Others often notice (somewhat recklessly) how much we are alike, and how much we have in common with both Mom and Dad, and now even with our own grown children. At one point I was confused, because I thought I was talking to my brother on the phone, when in fact I was speaking with his oldest son. When I openly confessed that I could not tell their voices apart, my brother readily conceded that he could not distinguish my voice from that of my youngest son. The unavoidable truth is that we are all very, very much alike. Our differences are important, and valuable, and essential not only to our self-understanding but also to our distinct usefulness. We play different roles and serve different purposes. And perhaps, if I may simply point at a mystery which I cannot yet grasp, the conflict between us has contributed to the precision of our distinctiveness, to our unique understanding of each other, and to our imperfect ability to work and function together as brothers, whether we find ourselves on opposite sides of the planet, or merely on either side of our mother, walking with her as one.

The most beautiful harmony I have ever heard was a trio of ladies in our community Tree of Life singing "Rose of Bethlehem", *a cappella* (without instruments). Technically, they were singing under my direction, but I did little more than persuade them to sing together, then point my baton at them when it was time to start. I knew the ladies well enough to know they had something of a complex history with each other. (In such a small town, everybody does.) I honestly don't know how much they practiced, or how difficult it might have been for each of them to get their parts just right, or blended just right with the others. I was with them during some of their practice, but I don't remember offering anything but affirmation. They knew each other well. They knew each other's strengths and weaknesses, confidence and fears, motivations and irritations. They knew what to say to each other, and how to say it. And yes, they knew how to get on each other's nerves, if that's what they wanted or needed to do.

When the rehearsals were over, the spotlight focused, and the audience prepared, I pointed my baton... and was lifted by the most beautiful vocal blend I have ever heard. Sometimes at night, now ten years later, as I drift off to sleep, I can still hear it echoing in the recesses of my memory, as ethereal and pure as ever. Looking back, I think perhaps it was more than just their voices that they learned to blend. I suspect they somehow cultivated harmony within their souls.

SYMPHONY: THE NEED FOR BELONGING

Today was a day that I did not want to be alone.

Mondays I typically have the office to myself. Other staff members are working from home, or at our customer's site, or working a part-time schedule that doesn't include Mondays. I use Mondays to focus, to organize my thoughts and my collection of transient writings on whiteboards. The rest and recuperation from the weekend gives me both energy and perspective needed to redraw connections and rethink priorities. It gives me a chance to work alone and undistracted on complex efforts that require undivided attention, to think deeply and ponder strategically. I sometimes love the tranquil solitude of Mondays. Today I despised it.

I think it started with an email from the director of the funeral home, received on Friday. He had heard back from Arlington National Cemetery, with a date available for my father's burial. One month from today... surprisingly soon, considering the normal wait of three to six months. It might give my brother and his wife an unexpected opportunity to be there for the ceremony, before they return to their mission work overseas. I was waiting to hear back from him, and Arlington needed an answer by 3pm today. I distracted myself with work, and then called again. He answered this time, and was pleased to know that the opportunity was offered. We will be together again a month from today, honoring my father and his dedicated service, saying goodbye once again.

When we hung up the phone, I was alone again. My mind went to close friends who have lost their fathers, some rather recently. That common grief, that familiarity of sorrow has wrapped an unexpectedly strong band around our friendships. It is a fraternity which I had no desire to join, yet which offers a silent network of understanding in which I find security. The circumstances of loss may be as distinct as our fingerprints, yet the shared significance of loss binds us in unspoken solidarity.

There are times when you simply want to be in the presence of people who have struggled as you are struggling, who have felt what you are feeling, whose mere existence gives testimony to the possibility of sufficient strength and endurance. Even in a room by myself, in a building otherwise unoccupied, I believe that I sensed their company, and their companionship.

I don't actually believe that there is anyone quite like me. I feel odd in that way, either slightly defective or simply divergent from the norm. On a very good day, I feel exceptional; on the other days, I just feel strange. Emotional pain has the remarkable power to remind us of just how much we have in common.

There are others who know what this feels like, whose feet have met this trail before mine did. I even sense that this particular sorrow — if I don't suppress it too much — will make me more alert and more receptive to others who have walked this way before me... and who will pass this way all too soon after.

There is another phenomenon of this uninvited unity, one which I can only express by returning again to the transcendent dynamics of music. My favorite song to play, without hesitation, is "Dueling Banjos". Yes, it's hard to find two banjo players of comparable skill in the same place at the same time who can pull off this energetic battle of bluegrass runs... but when you can, it can be magical.

Banjo players can often recognize each other before they've been introduced, even without the distinctive round-ended carrying case. There is something about the disposition, the shy confidence, the fast-fingered focus, the 22-fret versatility that shows up in the eyes and the set of the chin. And when you meet a banjo player who can match you note for note, with speed and agility, style and substance, you have made a friend and an ally, one who will have your back when the hordes of six-string box strummers storm the stage and surround all the microphones.

It is very, very good to have even one fellow traveler, who knows both the challenge of your trail and the weight of your burden. I don't know of any composer of any symphony who has ever scored a part for a banjo section, but I can assure you that if such a work were written, the banjos would own the hall. We are good at what we do, we don't mind being outnumbered, and we simply cannot hide the unique exuberance of our beloved instrument. We each have our own style, and will likely never play a piece exactly the same way as any of our peers, but as a group, we know that we are unmatched and inimitable.

The security, confidence, and pride that come from belonging to a strong and cohesive group is unlike any other human bond. The beautiful paradox that we are actually not alone in our uniqueness can conquer our most troubling fears and prepare our joints and sinews for even greater strains. We find great strength in unity, and we find great unity in shared passions and common struggles.

Even beyond that... rather far beyond that... the security of cohesive belonging enables us to embrace a broader diversity, and to find less obvious connections with people who have vastly different traits. The violinists who hold each other's trust are better prepared to interact with violas, cellos, and even those rather odd double-basses. The gathered sections of strings are secure enough in their own scores to welcome the proximity of brass and woodwinds, perhaps even enough to still their bows in humble silence, while the brash trumpets and flighty piccolos compete to draw all attention to themselves. If I may stretch this ideal to its logical extreme, the integrated groups of well-grounded sections in a mature, balanced orchestra can even rejoice at the overpowering thrust and imposing energy of an inspired band of percussionists, without losing the treasured value of their own instruments or the loyal bonds of their own sections.

This is symphony: the capacity to find strength, loyalty, and a corporate beauty of expression among increasingly large and diverse groups, still connected by common themes, a shared orchestration, and a contagious passion for the musical majesty of the whole.

The scars which we accumulate —from traversing briar patches, stumbling over sharp stones, or falling out of trees or burning airplanes — our visible and hidden wounds form the points of powerful connection with others like ourselves. You may have learned to see in the eyes of strangers that remnant of pain that is strikingly like your own. The more deeply familiar you are with the unique score of your own emotional journey, the more opportunity you will find to connect with those who have walked similar paths. And the stronger the bonds of those connections grow, the more ready and willing you will find yourself to share deep truths with people very unlike yourself. And the more diverse your shared connections, built on the foundation of your most faithful loyalties, the more rich and full and vibrant your experience will be of the symphonic orchestration of life itself.

Today was not a good day for me to be alone. Now, late at the end of that day and early at the beginning of another one, I find it somewhat surprising that I am not alone at all. I am surrounded by souls seen and unseen, who know both my journey and very different journeys, and who enrich my life with the unique expressions of experience very similar to and very different from my own.

COMMUNITY: THE POWER OF BINDING

The trip is just over an hour. It is about 70 miles from our house to the house my wife grew up in, where her parents still live, where we still gather with her brothers and our families each Thanksgiving, just like this one, and then again on Christmas Eve. The house is one that I have known — and felt welcome in — for longer than I have known my wife, for I knew her family before I knew her. (In fact, it was there that I first saw her, even before I knew her name.) The warm inviting home sits atop Eagle Hill, very near the center of a very small town, where time has not quite stood still, but slowed to a leisurely stroll that allows moments to linger and memories to endure.

To the young man in the back seat, with ear buds silently piping energetic songs into his otherwise relaxed mind, it is indeed another welcome trip to grandmother's house. (It is of course grandfather's house as well.) Over three rivers we cross on the way: the Kentucky, the Salt, and the Chaplin. The woods we pass through are many and nameless to most, cleared in part some 50 years ago, enough to make room for the wide parkway that now makes our journey easy and smooth. It is essentially the same journey, and the same 70 miles, made 70 years ago by my wife's mother's parents, when they transplanted a large cluster of family roots from where they had long been to where they now strongly hold.

Along the way we pass the place where my wife used to work, the baseball fields where her son sometimes played, the soccer field where my oldest son practiced, the high school my wife and my sons all graduated from, decades apart and long before she and I met. We pass the house where I used to live, homes and farms that belong or belonged to various friends and acquaintances — some that we both have known, some familiar to only one of us. The roads and places are very much part of both of our histories, but the timelines of those histories diverge and converge in ways that lead us frequently to ask, "Did you know the people who used to live there?" Even when the answer is "yes", we often knew them at different times in different ways, and our perspectives enhance each other's understanding, even of people we each know well.

I shudder slightly when we pass the intersection where a young couple crashed 25 years ago. Theirs was the first wedding I had performed, and their five-month old son was critically injured in the crash. All survived, but I will never forget the anxious hours in the hospital waiting room. The couple was so young that the hospital staff barely acknowledged them as the infant's terrified parents. An unexpected piece of my pastoral role was finding a doctor who could simply tell mom and dad if their baby boy would be okay. He had suffered injuries to his skull, and there was great cause for concern that extended for weeks and months. With the passage of time and provision of care, the wounds of child and parents all healed, leaving behind only scars — lasting signs of pain endured and crisis overcome.

From my in-laws' driveway atop Eagle Hill, as the trees have lost their autumn leaves, we can clearly see the expansive roof of the Methodist church, where the Tree of Life stood every Christmas season for 25 years. We can see most of the town from there, and the sights and memories weave past and present into a warm and familiar quilt. My wife and I survey the horizon side by side, and speak briefly of the possibility of living there again someday, perhaps in that house right there, just across the highway, or maybe in the one at the bottom of the hill, with the "For Sale by Owner" sign.

Inside the house, the warm smile of my father-in-law steps gently into the cold shadow left by my own father's passing. I want to give him a long bear hug, but I know he is more comfortable with a firm handshake, and a spark exchanged with the eyes that reaches deep into the soul. My mother-in-law is anxious as always to ensure everyone immediately has everything they want, and we do our best to assure her that our needs are well met, even more by shared presence than by the wonderful food and drink generously offered.

We are joined by the happy newlyweds, my wife's daughter and her husband, having returned only last night from their honeymoon adventure out west. Stories and pictures are eagerly received, even as the realization crystallizes that they now form their own family, within the larger family. We even detect the faint hint of children in their thoughts, who will someday become welcomed and loved grandchildren, great-grandchildren, nieces, nephews, and second cousins to the others gathered here.

My brother-in-law shares a few tales of his own adventures, with a gift for storytelling that unfailingly evokes joy and laughter, even if the story has been told several times before. It is a gift he received well from his father, one of the master weavers of tales tall and short that I have ever known. At one wonderful point, father and son join together to tell one familiar favorite, with seamless transitions between their charm and wit as the story unfolds along its well-known route.

My stepson and I share a story or two as well, to contribute what we can. We share briefly from our trip last weekend, back to my hometown, to the immense stadium filled with football fanatics clad in orange, singing and screaming "Rocky Top" to the limits of their vocal range. A nostalgic walk through that campus had triggered long-faded memories of friends and extended family, adventures and minor crises, distant fears and dreams. It was good to have someone to share those memories with, both then and again now, even as new enduring memories are being formed.

I'm running out of words to describe the intricate web of connections — of people and places, of memories behind and hopes ahead — that form the fabric of this singular Thanksgiving Day. There something wonderfully magical about this place, which is deeply intertwined with the many wonderful people who live and gather here, who have gathered here for many reasons through many years.

Like the twine that binds countless bales of hay across vast fields at autumn harvest, so the strings that hold faith and family, care and community are mostly imperceptible, except by their effect. We may not be aware of exactly what it is that binds us together, but we sense with growing conviction that we are somehow together tightly bound. We belong to each other; we live for each other. Every experience and every expression of thought and feeling is somehow incomplete until it is shared, and it is shared most fully and completely within community.

Communities crystallize significance and communicate meaning far beyond anything we can ever express on our own. Echoes of ancestry and shared history hold harmonic resonance longer than any solitary life will last. The stories we share become parts of other stories, told by other voices, conveying joys and truths far beyond any that we ourselves can truly know.

You are wonderfully composed. Share your wonder. Tell your stories. Express your thoughts. Give sound and voice to the full range of your emotional experience. Do so with transparent authenticity, without deception or guile, so that others might have opportunity to learn what you have learned. Do so with genuine sensitivity, without judgement or offense, so that your gifts might transcend your own limitations. Indeed, your compositions shall live longer than you do, and they will impact unseen networks of communities, beyond anything you can now count or imagine.

www.ingramcontent.com/pod-product-compliance
Lightning Source LLC
Chambersburg PA
CBHW071449080526
44587CB00014B/2042